GUATEMALA
Central America's Living Past

AMERICA GOES TO THE FAIR
All About State and County Fairs in the USA

EAST AFRICA, Kenya, Tanzania
Uganda

EATING THE VEGETARIAN WAY
Good Food From the Earth

EGYPT
Rebirth on the Nile

GHANA AND IVORY COAST
Spotlight on West Africa

THE GLOBAL FOOD SHORTAGE
Food Scarcity on Our Planet and What We Can Do About It

MEXICO
Crucible of the Americas

PUERTO RICO
Island Between Two Worlds

GUATEMALA
Central America's Living Past

LILA PERL

illustrated with photographs

William Morrow and Company   New York   1982

Printed in the United States of America.
1 2 3 4 5 6 7 8 9 10

Library of Congress Cataloging in Publication Data

Perl, Lila.
  Guatemala, Central America's living past.

  Bibliography: p. 154
  Includes index.
  Summary: Describes the history, politics, economic situation, and social life of Guatemala and assesses its role in the present instability of Central America.
  1. Guatemala—Juvenile literature. [1. Guatemala] I. Title.
F1463.2.P47   972.81   81-18782
ISBN 0-688-01073-3   AACR2

ACKNOWLEDGMENTS

The author wishes to express her gratitude to the following for their cooperation and assistance:

Lic. Alvaro Arzú, Director, Instituto Guatemalteco de Turismo; Claire Mangers, M. Silver Associates, Inc., New York City; Lou Hammond, Pan American World Airways; Ana Smith, President, Panamundo Guatemala Travel Service; Fernando Taque, Manager, Panamundo Guatemala Travel Service; Leif Ness; Mario Soto; Nicky Smith, Textile Curator, Ixchel Museum; Popol Vuh Museum; Jane Ragsdale, *The Guatemala News;* John Montgomery

Courtesies extended by the following are acknowledged with appreciation: William Jauregui, Jr., Camino Real Hotel, Guatemala City; Kevin Lucas, Catamarán Island Hotel, Río Dulce; Pan American Hotel, Guatemala City; Maya International Hotel, Flores

All photographs are by Lila Perl with the exception of the following from the United Nations: pp. 122 (Y. Nagata), 127, 131, 133 (Y. Nagata), 143 (T. Chen), 145, 147 (Jerry Frank), 150 (Saw Lwin). Permission is gratefully acknowledged.

Contents

1

Land of the Quetzal

In the cool, misty heights of Guatemala's cloud forest dwells the quetzal (ket-ZAHL), the sacred bird of the ancient Maya and the symbol of liberty of modern Guatemala. Today few people ever see a living specimen of this legendary bird with its crimson breast and long, iridescent green tail feathers. It survives hidden and protected in the lush mountain greenery of Alta Verapaz, one of the twenty-two departments, or provinces, of Guatemala.

The cloud forest is home, too, to the *monja blanca,* or white nun, a richly delicate white orchid that is the national flower of Guatemala. Yet this lofty climate zone of softly dripping woodlands is not at all typical of the country as a whole.

Guatemala, which is only about the size of the state of Ohio, is almost as varied in its topography, temperature, and rainfall as Mexico, its neighbor to the north and west. Yet Guatemala is just 42,042 square miles in area, about one-eighteenth the size of Mexico.

Geographers tell us that the snakelike land bridge that connects North and South America really begins at the "narrow waist" of Mexico, known as the Isthmus of Tehuantepec. It then curves in a southeasterly direction all the way to Colombia on the northwestern shoulder of South America. The portion of this writhing neck of land that we call Central America consists

In Guatemala's cloud forest, the preserve of the quetzal

11

principally of five sovereign countries, of which Guatemala is the northernmost.

On Guatemala's southeast border lie Honduras and tiny El Salvador. Beyond Honduras, also to the southeast, are Nicaragua and finally Costa Rica. The Pacific Ocean washes the southwestern coast of Guatemala, and the Caribbean Sea, a basin of the Atlantic Ocean, bathes a small section of northeastern Guatemala.

Two countries that are also located on the Central American isthmus, but historically have not been considered part of its family of nations, are Panama and Belize. Panama, which was part of Colombia until 1903, is still regarded by many as a northwesterly extension of South America, while Belize, which lies directly to the east of Guatemala, was until 1981 a British possession. From 1862 to 1973, it was known as British Honduras. For geographic, historic, and political reasons, Guatemala has never ceased to claim Belize as part of Guatemalan territory, and maps printed in Guatemala show "Belice" as its twenty-third department.

The outline of Guatemala's internationally recognized boundaries, as seen on the map, resembles that of a visored sentinel, its profile facing west. And indeed this nation does seem to stand guard at the gateway to all of Central America over which it once held considerable sway. Topographically Guatemala still dominates the isthmus, for it has the highest volcanic peaks, many of them thrusting up to 10,000 to 14,000 feet. Its major chain of mountains, a continuation of the mighty Sierra Madre range of Mexico, runs on in broken ridges all the way to Costa Rica, which with its 12,000-foot peaks is the second highest country in Central America. The highest point on the isthmus is the Tajumulco volcano (13,846 feet) in western Guatemala, in the department of San Marcos.

UNITED STATES

Gulf of Mexico

CUBA

*Yucatán
Peninsula*

MEXICO

TABASCO

JAMAICA

*Isthmus of
Tehuantepec*

BELIZE

CHIAPAS

Caribbean Sea

GUATEMALA

HONDURAS

EL SALVADOR

NICARAGUA

Pacific Ocean

COSTA RICA

Panama Canal

*Gulf of
Darien*

PANAMA

COLOMBIA

CENTRAL AMERICA

MEXICO

• El Mirador

• Palenque

• Uaxactún
• Tikal

• Piedras Negras

Lake Petén Itzá

BELIZE

FLORES

MEXICO

Río de la Pasión

EL PETÉN

Ceibal

Caribbean

HUEHUETENANGO

ALTA VERAPAZ

Bay of Amatique

• Lívingston

IZABAL

PUERTO BARRIOS

QUICHÉ

San Pedro Carchá

Todos Santos Cuchumatán

Santo Tomás de Castilla

Río Dulce

HUEHUETENANGO

• Nebaj

COBÁN

Lake Izabal

Río Polochic

SAN MARCOS

SANTA CRUZ DEL QUICHÉ

Quiriguá

BAJA VERAPAZ

Tajumulco (13,846 ft.)

Río Motagua

SAN MARCOS

Chichicastenango

SALAMÁ

ZACAPA

• Copán

SANTA CRUZ DEL QUICHÉ

EL PROGRESO

ZACAPA

HONDURAS

Lake Atitlán

GUATEMALA

EL PROGRESO

CHIQUIMULA

RETALHULEU

MAZATENANGO

GUATEMALA CITY

JALAPA

CHIQUIMULA

RETALHULEU

Lake Amatitlán

Palín

JALAPA

Esquipulas

SUCHITEPÉQUEZ

ESCUINTLA

CUILAPA

JUTIAPA

La Democracia

SANTA ROSA

JUTIAPA

ESCUINTLA

Puerto San José

EL SALVADOR

Pacific Ocean

GUATEMALA
AND ITS DEPARTMENTS

Momostenango

TOTONICAPÁN
TOTONICAPÁN

Quezaltenango

SOLOLÁ
SOLOLÁ

Iximché
Tecpán

QUEZALTENANGO

Panajachel

Patzún

CHIMALTENANGO

SACATEPÉQU

Lake Atitlán

Patzicía
CHIMALTENANGO

Santiago
Sacatepéqu

Santiago Atitlán

ANTIGUA

Ciudad Vieja

Land of the Quetzal

The mountains that cover two-thirds of Guatemala are a mixed blessing. They afford a cool, springlike year-round climate in a latitude that, at sea level, is apt to be tropically hot and steamy. In fact, Guatemala's predominantly high terrain of 5000 feet and more has earned it the name of El País de Eterna Primavera, the Land of Eternal Spring. But the steep, jagged character of the mountains has also made farming difficult and has divided

Below: One of Guatemala's several hundred volcanoes, 12,000-foot-high Agua, seen from the market square in the village of Palín

the country into isolated pockets of civilization cut off from communication with one another and the world beyond. The same has been true for much of the rest of Central America.

A striking replica of Guatemala's topography is seen in the unique Relief Map of sculptured concrete that was laid out in 1905 in Minerva Park, on the northern edge of Guatemala City, the nation's capital. The map, which takes up almost half a city block, gives a detailed view with place names of the country's mountains, lakes, rivers, coastal plains, and jungle region. There are even ponds representing the Pacific Ocean and the Caribbean Sea, the latter showing the islands of the long barrier reefs that lie off the coast of Belize. To conserve space, the vertical scale of the map is somewhat exaggerated, giving the taller volcanic

The Relief Map showing Lake Izabal, the Río Dulce, and the Caribbean Sea

peaks a dramatic, needlelike appearance. The architect of the Relief Map was Francisco Vela, a Guatemalan Army officer and engineer.

Startling changes occur as one descends by hairpin turns from the temperate and sometimes chilly highland zones of western and central Guatemala to the Pacific coastal plain, the Caribbean lowlands, or the vast northern jungle of the department of El Petén. The temperature rises with each succeeding drop in altitude, stalwart pine trees give way to feathery coconut palms, and temperate-zone crops like corn, beans, and apples are replaced by tropical fruits as well as agricultural products raised for export. The level Pacific plain, once the site of indigo and cacao plantations, is now devoted to growing sugarcane, cotton, and rice, and it has also become the center of the cattle-raising industry. Coffee, which grows well in Guatemala over a broad range of altitudes, from 800 to 6000 feet, is cultivated on the upper Pacific slopes. The Pacific shore itself is rimmed with beaches of black volcanic sand that bake beneath a fiery sun during the long dry season.

Much wetter the year round is the Caribbean coastal area. Most of Guatemala's banana plantations are now located in this region. Here, too, is the Lago de Izabal, Guatemala's largest lake, which is fed by the Río Polochic with tributaries arising in the mountains of the department of Alta Verapaz. The waters of Lake Izabal flow into the Caribbean via the Río Dulce, or Sweet River, a broad, gentle stream. The river is bordered by verdant cliffs, their rich vegetation of leafy boughs and vines gracefully overhanging its banks.

The densest vegetation, however, is found in the northern third of Guatemala, a limestone plain that rolls on northward into the somewhat drier Yucatán peninsula of Mexico. Flying low over Guatemala's Petén, one gazes down upon a landscape that looks like a sea of furry green pimples. They are the tops of the mahogany, cedar, palm, and ceiba trees that flourish, among many others, in this well-watered region. The ceiba is also named the kapok, or silk-cotton, tree, because it produces a seedpod of fluffy fibers that can be used as mattress and pillow stuffing. Much favored by Guatemalans because it can grow to enormous girth, the ceiba tree is often planted for shade in town plazas around the country.

Most typical of the Petén jungle is the sapodilla, or chicle, tree, which yields a gummy latex that is tapped from its bark. During the latter half of the nineteenth century, this substance became commercially important as the principal ingredient of chewing gum. Since about 1950, however, synthetic gums have become more common. Two popular Guatemalan fruits that come from trees of the sapodilla family are the sapote and the chicozapote. Both have rough, potato-brown skins that peel easily. The flesh of the sapote is a deep apricot color, smooth, velvety, and deliciously sweet. The chicozapote, a smaller fruit, is paler-fleshed, juicier, and slightly grainy.

Sparsely populated today, with a density of only one and a half persons per square mile, the Petén was once the site of the great stone ceremonial centers of the Mayan Indians. Each of these centers was supported by a large population. In recent years, oil has been discovered in the southern portion of the Petén, which promises to bring some renewed activity to that sector.

At present, most of the inhabitants of the Petén are clustered around Lake Petén Itzá, which lies almost at the center of the department. Its capital and best-known town, Flores, is built on a cone-shaped island connected to the shore by a causeway. According to an Indian legend, Lake Petén Itzá is believed to rise every fifty years, and in the early 1930's and again in the early 1980's it appeared to have fulfilled that prophecy. Fed by pro-

An excavated palace at Tikal in the dense Petén jungle

longed rains, the lake overflowed its shores in 1980-1981 and inundated many small lakeside communities, which had to be evacuated. Flores itself was cut off from the mainland and could be reached only by boat.

Two other lakes of note in Guatemala are Lake Atitlán, in the highlands west of Guatemala City, and Lake Amatitlán, a short distance south of the capital. Lake Atitlán, 5200 feet above sea level, is of volcanic origin, and its waters, more than 1000 feet deep in some places, are shadowed by volcanic peaks that soar to nearly 12,000 feet. Indian villages dot the shoreline and *cayucos*, or dugout canoes, their sides built up with extra wooden planks, are used for fishing. But although the lake yields several varieties

19

An Indian fisherman on Lake Atitlán

of table fish, most inhabitants rely mainly on farming. The lake is roughened each afternoon when a wind known as the *xocomil* (sho-ko-MEEL) sweeps in from between the surrounding mountains. Few Indians learn to swim, and many seem reluctant to invade the lake because of the belief that spirits inhabit its waters.

The much smaller Lake Amatitlán is also volcanic. Like Atitlán, it rests in a collapsed volcano, known as a caldera. The proximity of Pacaya, an active volcano, contributes to the presence of bubbling hot springs near the lake. As it is only about fifteen miles from the congested metropolis of Guatemala City, Lake Amatitlán serves as a weekend resort and vacation destination for city dwellers. It has a public beach and many private lakeside cottages, but unfortunately its waters have become polluted in recent years with sewage and industrial wastes.

Directly to the east of Guatemala City lies Oriente, a region that is very different from the Indian-inhabited western highlands. If the temperate highlands can be compared to New England, particularly Vermont and New Hampshire, Oriente almost resembles the American Southwest.

The long valley of the Motagua River, about five miles wide and hemmed in by mountains, is arid and dotted with scrub growth and cactus, especially the long-armed candelabra variety. Oriente was settled in Spanish colonial times by small landowners who thoughtlessly stripped the trees, causing erosion and contributing to the soil impoverishment of the region. Tobacco and some other crops grown in Oriente are irrigated with water diverted from the Motagua River. The grazing cattle have large, fatty neck humps. They are of the Brahman, or zebu, type, a breed that is resistant to heat and drought.

The dryness of the Motagua valley is due to the Sierra de las Minas, the mountain range that borders it on the north and blocks off the trade winds that blow from the northeast. On the other side of the Sierra the climate is moist: tropical in the lowlands of the department of Izabal, and cool and wet in the highlands, as in the cloud forest of Alta Verapaz.

Guatemalans are fond of saying that they have only two seasons, a wet season lasting from May to October or November and a dry season from December to April. But there are exceptions like the Petén and the Caribbean lowlands, where rainfall can continue well into the dry months, and Alta Verapaz, where even in January and February there is an imperceptible but saturating drizzle that local people call the *chipi chipi*. In most of the country, however, the wet-season rains consist of only an hour or two of heavy showers daily in the afternoon.

The arrival of the dry season with its clear skies and fresh breezes is so welcomed that Guatemalans commonly refer to it as *verano*, or summer, even though technically it is winter in the northern hemisphere. The rainy season, although it is accompanied by somewhat warmer temperatures, is considered Guatemala's *invierno*, or winter.

The factor that most determines temperature, however, is altitude. At sea level to 2500 feet, one is in the *tierra caliente*, or "hot land," with daytime readings of 80 to 90 degrees Fahrenheit and nights only a little cooler. The *tierra templada*, or "temperate land," of 2500 to 5500 feet brings temperatures in the sixties and seventies, with an average of 68 degrees Fahrenheit. The *tierra fría*, "cold land" of 5500 to 12,000 feet, and the *tierra helada*, "frozen land" of 12,000 feet and over, bring progressively colder weather and even snow. In the western highland departments of Quezaltenango and Huehuetenango, at 7000 to 9000 feet, the temperature can drop to the twenties and thirties in December, as cold as it is in New York. Even in Guatemala City, which has an altitude of 5000 feet, the saying that "night is the winter of the tropics" holds true. Residents who dress in short sleeves and even sunbacks during the day may don boots and fur or quilted jackets in the evenings and early mornings.

Throughout Guatemala and the rest of Central America, the presence of shifting plates of Earth's crust has repeatedly caused volcanic eruptions and earthquakes. In fact, almost all of Middle America, extending from Mexico to Costa Rica, is what geologists call "an active mountain-building region" because of its volcanic character.

No sooner had the sixteenth-century Spanish conquerors of Guatemala built their early capital, today known as Ciudad

A vendor in San Pedro Carchá in Alta Verapaz, land of the *chipi chipi*

23

Vieja, than a series of earth tremors caused the water-filled crater of the extinct volcano Agua to inundate the colonial city with an avalanche of water, rocks, and mud, utterly destroying it in 1541. Antigua, the next capital, was devastated by a disastrous earthquake in 1773. And the present capital has received major shocks in 1917, 1918, and 1976. The massive quake of February 4, 1976 cut a broad swathe across the country. Most of the 25,000 deaths took place in the department of Chimaltenango to the west of the capital. Many thousands of those left homeless set up squatters' shelters of planks and corrugated tin, precariously perched atop the *barrancos,* or canyons, on the northern edge of Guatemala City.

Even today in Guatemala City only a small number of modern earthquake-proof office blocks and hotels are multistoried. Most structures are a single story high and built of cement-plastered brick. Corrugated metal roofing has replaced most of the attractive but hazardous tile roofing of the colonial buildings that crashed down and killed so many inhabitants in 1917 and 1918.

Earthquake activity in Guatemala never really stops. In 1980 alone, over one hundred and seventy tremors, although none of great severity, were registered in various parts of the country. The same is true elsewhere in Central America. There the worst earthquake to occur in recent years was the one that destroyed Nicaragua's capital of Managua in 1972.

Of Guatemala's several hundred volcanoes, those that are notably active, belching smoke and occasionally spewing lava and ash, are Pacaya near Lake Amatitlán, Fuego near Antigua, and the Santiaguito crater of Santa María near Quezaltenango, Gua-

Fuego, on the left, an active volcano that looms over the village of Alotenango near Antigua

temala's second largest city. In the violent eruption of Santa María in 1902, 6000 people died. While many of Guatemala's volcanoes are extinct, the number of those that are potentially active is unknown.

Despite its challenging terrain and untamable natural forces, Central America effectively served as a land bridge for a migrating stream of animals, people, and plant life in ages past. The wide variety of birds and other animals now found on the isthmus shows it to be a meeting place for adapted species of both temperate and tropical climes. Among Guatemala's four hundred resident birds are both the everyday robin and the rare quetzal. There are grackles, wrens, and crows, as well as brilliantly plumaged toucans and macaws.

Opossums and squirrels, familiar in North America, exist alongside monkeys, kinkajous, coatis, and iguanas. Among larger animals are the deer, the peccary, a type of wild pig, and the tapir, a gentle, long-snouted animal distantly related to the horse and the rhinoceros. Predatory beasts include the jaguar, ocelot, and puma. The cayman and the closely related alligator lurk in the swampy coastal waters. It is said that the manatee, or sea cow, was formerly found in Lake Izabal, and dolphins gambol to this day in the unspoiled Río Dulce.

Human beings first arrived in the western hemisphere from Asia. Their route was via a narrow land bridge that, during the Ice Age, spanned the Bering Strait. Later, when the ice cap melted, the seas rose and cut off further land contact with the eastern hemisphere. America's human inhabitants are believed to have appeared between 20,000 and 50,000 years ago and to have reached the isthmus of Central America no later than 12,000 years ago.

A pair of macaws, members of the brilliantly plumaged parrot family

The cultivation of the wild edible plant that came to be known as maize, or Indian corn, is thought to have begun in central Mexico around 5000 B.C. People who had long been hunters and gatherers gradually became settled maize-growing agriculturalists. Pottery finds in Central America dating from about 2000 B.C. tell us that a farming society organized into village life must have existed by then.

Principal among the Indian peoples of Middle America were the Maya, whose civilization, although centered in Guatemala, fanned out into the surrounding territory of the Mexican state of Chiapas and the Yucatán peninsula, as well as to neighboring El Salvador, Honduras, and Belize. Although many other Indian groups occupied the Central American isthmus, none developed a society as rich in artistic and scientific achievement as the Mayas, and none have carried their ancient beliefs and way of life into the modern era as faithfully.

Most of the non-Mayan Indians of coastal and southern Central America were not primarily growers of maize. Their staples, like those of the inhabitants of the Caribbean islands and of northern South America, were starchy tubers—the sweet potato, arrowroot, and manioc, or cassava—all of which grew best in the humid lowlands. They also depended strongly on hunting and fishing. Among the few identifiable surviving groups are the Cuna Indians of the San Blas Islands, located off the Caribbean coast of Panama.

Within the borders of Guatemala, one can trace the development of the Maya from their beginnings to their period of greatest grandeur and on to the time of the Spanish conquest. The Pacific lowlands appear to have nourished the Mayan civilization in its infancy. Partly buried amidst the dense growth of today's sugarcane fields have been found an assortment of crude to refined stone sculptures. Some were roughly incised on huge boulders of basalt while others were skillfully carved or hewn into fully rounded figures.

In the hot, sleepy town plaza of La Democracia in southern Guatemala, the sketchily engraved sculptures called the "fat boys" are displayed, shaded by a giant ceiba tree. Some of the rotund shapes represent entire torsos while others are devoted solely to heads. Most have frowning but not menacing expressions. Do these bulbous rocks represent fertility? And does the recent discovery of natural magnetic poles at the navels and temples of the carved figures indicate some connection with the idea of the life-force?

Another matter that puzzles archeologists is the resemblance of the fat boys to similar carvings of the Olmecs, whose civilization flourished around 1000 B.C. in Mexico, in the state of Tabasco. As the La Democracia carvings may possibly date from

A crudely carved stone head at La Democracia

as long ago as 2000 B.C., it is thought possible that a pre-Olmec people were the common ancestors of both the Maya and such distant cousins as the Olmec-descended Zapotecs of Mexico. Theories and rough guesses abound, for the dating of the pre-Mayan and early Mayan sculptures is highly uncertain.

About 2500 years ago, 500 years before the birth of Christ, some Mayan groups appear to have migrated northward and to have begun establishing ceremonial and residential cities in the highlands. One such city was Kaminaljuyú, the Hill of the Dead. Located on what was once the western fringe of Guatemala City, this important archeological find is now surrounded by a modern residential neighborhood. On the site itself, however, grassy hillocks and mounds of earth attest to the presence of stepped platforms once crowned with temples. Excavations have revealed that there were burial crypts beneath the temple platforms, and they have yielded pottery, jewelry, tools, incense burners, and other artifacts now on exhibit in the city's museums.

Wandering around Kaminaljuyú, one's interest is piqued by the easy finds of small shards of ancient pottery mixed with the soil and bits of shaped obsidian, the smoky dark-gray volcanic glass that the Maya worked into keen-bladed knives. Treasures still lie underground, particularly beneath the pavements of the encroaching city streets. They could tell us a great deal more about this preclassic center, which throve shortly before the Mayan civilization burst into the splendor of its classic period, which lasted from A.D. 300 to 900.

For some time before A.D. 300, for reasons unknown, the Maya had been leaving their highland cities like Kaminaljuyú and descending into the lowland jungle of the Petén. Were the

A skillful Mayan engraving from the Pacific lowlands
showing a jaguar-headed conqueror

highland plateaus becoming too crowded? Was there too little rainfall to grow enough corn for an expanding population? As might be expected, some groups stayed behind just as others had remained behind in the Pacific area hundreds, even thousands, of years earlier. But the main thrust of the Maya was jungleward, and clear proof of the dates involved has emerged because of the excellent numbering system the Mayans developed.

At Tikal, the great ceremonial city of the Petén, where the Maya built the tallest temple pyramids in the Americas, the earliest recorded date is A.D. 292. It appears on a stela, a tall stone panel carved with figures, hieroglyphs (picture writing), and numbering symbols. Stelae were customarily erected in the plazas of the religious centers to commemorate a particular event or time span, such as a lahuntun (ten years) or a katun (twenty years).

Because agriculture figured so importantly in Mayan life, observations of the rainy and dry seasons as they affected planting and harvesting were vital. As a result, an amazingly accurate calendar was established. It consisted of eighteen months of twenty days each, plus a short "month" of five days, totaling 365 days. The Mayans also devised a 260-day sacred calendar that is still observed by some Indian groups in Guatemala in connection with religious festivals. Also in use was a system called a "long count" for figuring time from a fixed date of creation. The Maya chose the equivalent of the year 3114 B.C., using it as a point of reference much as the Western world uses the date of the birth of Christ.

The mathematical and astronomical knowledge of the Mayas was extraordinary. They developed the concept of zero as early or earlier than the Hindus did. At that period in history, the classical civilizations of Greece and Rome were using the relatively clumsy Roman numerals. The Mayan numbering notations made use of dots and bars, a dot representing one and a bar five. In astronomy, eclipses of the sun and moon were accurately predicted, and the path of Venus was charted.

What scientists marvel at most today, however, are the imposing structures built at Tikal and other classic sites by this Stone Age people who did not have any wheeled vehicles, draft animals, or beasts of burden. In the Great Plaza at Tikal, two huge temple-topped pyramids of gray-white limestone stand facing each other across a grassy expanse. The Temple of the Giant Jaguar, known as Temple I, which can be ascended via a staircase of dizzying steepness, soars to a height of 145 feet. Opposite it stands the 125-foot Temple of the Masks, known as Temple II. In other locations at Tikal are its two tallest temples: the unexcavated Temple III, the Temple of the Jaguar Priest, 180 feet high, and Temple IV, the Temple of the Double-Headed Serpent, 212 feet high.

The pyramid base of Temple IV is buried and crumbling beneath a tall mound of earth covered with dense jungle foliage. But by clambering up through a tangle of tree roots and thick, woody vines, one can reach the temple, which has been restored. It consists of three rooms that once contained intricately carved wooden lintels. The lintels are now in a museum in Switzerland. Mayan temples, which usually have one to three thick-walled stone chambers, have often taken their names from the carvings found on their wooden beams of rot-proof sapodilla wood.

Archways, when they were built between the temple rooms, were of the corbel type: opposing blocks of stone placed closer and closer together until they could be capped by a single block. The Mayans did not know how to build the true, or keystone, arch developed by the Romans. Tall roof combs, walls arising from the temple roofs and faced with sculpted stucco, increased the awesome appearance of the Mayan temples.

Some of the pyramids, like that of Temple I, have been found to house funerary crypts. Apparently they were the burial places of important rulers, for they contained jewelry, handsomely decorated pottery, and other articles of value. The ruler entombed in Temple I was buried with 180 pieces of jade weighing a total of sixteen and a half pounds.

At its height, Tikal's religious center spanned many square miles and numbered thousands of structures that included palaces, platforms, astronomical observatories, ball courts, and sweat baths. There were numerous stelae and large drumlike offering stones that were almost certainly used for sacrificing

Reminders of the Mayan religion—
Left: The 145-foot Temple of the Giant Jaguar
(note staircase chain for climbers to grasp)
Below: An offering stone showing king and executioner
(note human leg bones piled horizontally near base)

human beings as well as animals. Although the Maya are thought of as an "enlightened" people because of their scientific and artistic accomplishments, they believed their gods to be thirsty for human blood and did not hesitate to put to death the bravest warriors and the most skilled athletes to appease that thirst.

Unlike the Aztecs of Mexico and the Incas of Peru, the Maya did not have a vast territorial empire that was centrally governed. Although culturally unified, they were divided into individually strong city-states of which Tikal is the best known in the Petén because of its extent, its majesty, and the large amount of restoration work done. Most recently, however, archeologists have begun to unearth a city called El Mirador, north of Tikal near the Mexican border. El Mirador, which seems to have flourished several hundred years earlier, is believed to have had at least one pyramid as tall or possibly even taller than those at Tikal and with a much broader base.

Other notable Mayan ceremonial centers contemporary with Tikal are Palenque, in the Mexican state of Chiapas, and Copán, just over the Guatemalan border in Honduras. At Copán, Mayan decorative art is richly expressed in the intricate and lavish carving of the stelae, temples, and pyramid stairways.

Within Guatemala's border, not very far from Copán, is Quiriguá, a site that shares some of the exquisitely realized decoration of Copán. Remains at Quiriguá, which must have been a small religious center, show that the temple plaza was minor. Outstanding, however, are the nine stelae and six zoomorphs (huge boulders roughly resembling crouching animals) of pinkish-brown sandstone that dot the parklike grounds, which are today surrounded by lush banana plantations.

A richly carved stela, twenty feet tall, at Quiriguá

The stelae, which include the tallest found on any Mayan site, are deeply carved on all four sides with great, looming figures of rulers, elaborate symbols and designs, and finely detailed glyphs. The zoomorphs are also fully engraved. Although only about 30 percent of all Mayan hieroglyphic writing has been deciphered, the dates on the monuments at Quiriguá have been worked out to the year, month, and day. Most date from the eighth century.

The soaring temples and pillars of the Mayan religious centers are monuments not only to the glorification of the gods, who presumably dwelt in the heavens, but also to the self-glorification of the ruling class. The Mayan form of government in the classic period was a theocracy, in which the ruler or rulers were also the religious authorities. Their power was absolute, for they themselves were considered to be, at the very least, semidivine. They, along with their retinues of civic, religious, and military officials, lived in the ceremonial centers, attended by staffs that saw to their personal needs.

What about the rest of the population, those who fashioned the tools of obsidian and flint, who quarried and transported the immense blocks of stone to build the pyramids, who painstakingly carved the temples, stelae, and altars, who crafted the fine jade, bone, shell, and featherwork ornaments with which the ruling class adorned itself? The common people, most of whom were farmers engaged in growing the food that supported Tikal and similar great cities, lived outside the religious center, in the surrounding countryside. When the farmer-laborers were not chopping away at brush and trees with a stone axe to clear a new milpa, or cornfield, they were likely prying slabs of stone from a

A zoomorph at Quiriguá
(note large upside-down Mayan profile in upper left quarter of picture)

distant quarry with poles and wedges of wood, lashing the stones to logs with strong cords of plant fiber, and laboriously rolling them to the new building site decreed by the current power elite.

Jungle agriculture was not easily accomplished. After being felled, the trees and woody underbrush were burned so that the fertilizing ash could enrich the soil. Crops could then be grown in it for a year or two. This method is known as slash-and-burn agriculture. However, once stripped of its natural cover, jungle soil was quickly depleted of nutrients. The field then had to be left to lie fallow for four to seven years, until new woody growth appeared and the process could be repeated. Meantime, the peasantry was kept busy clearing new fields in a never-ending cycle.

Despite the large amount of rainfall, irrigation too was a problem. Mayan ingenuity developed a system of terracing and canals, with water drawn from rivers and lagoons. A recent radar-testing survey over the Guatemalan rain forest revealed, quite by accident, that at some Mayan sites crops were grown on islandlike plots of rich soil thrown up from the irrigation ditches. The Aztecs of Mexico also cultivated food on raised fields, which they called "chinampas."

With the use of a dibble, or digging stick, a hole was made in the ground and the seed dropped in. Even the simple plow was unknown, nor would it have been of much use in the shallow, rocky soil without a draft animal to pull it. Weeding and harvesting were done by hand. In addition to corn, beans, and squash —the Indian staples known as the American trinity, which the Maya succeeded in adapting to the moist lowlands—the farmers grew chili peppers, tomatoes, avocados, papayas, and other fruits and vegetables. The breadnut, picked from the jungle-growing ramon tree, provided a mealy substance from which a kind of bread could be baked. Turkeys were raised for the table, and deer and other forest animals were trapped for food. Bees provided honey and wax. Gourds were grown to serve as cups and bowls.

Trade was of vital importance in the life of Tikal. Obsidian, flint, and volcanic stones for grinding dried, soaked corn into masa (the "dough" from which tortillas are baked) came from the highlands, as did precious jade. This green-to-black gemstone was worked into jewelry and other articles for the very rich, who even had the outer surfaces of their teeth drilled with holes into which mosaics of jade were fitted.

Cacao beans, which came all the way from the Pacific lowlands, are believed to have been used at times as currency, while salt, dried fish, ornamental shells, and sting-ray spines had to be brought from the seacoasts. The needlelike spines were used by priests and rulers to pierce their ears, lips, tongues, and even genitals. It is believed that the self-inflicted pain was intended to induce a kind of religious ecstasy.

Other types of mutilation were practiced. The Maya favored a sloping forehead and crossed eyes, which, along with a prominent nose, they regarded as the ideal of beauty. To produce these features, they flattened the foreheads of their infants by binding them between boards and hung dangling beads before their eyes causing them to cross. Affluent adults had holes drilled in their septums and earlobes so that they could wear costly nose ornaments and large heavy earplugs. Front teeth, in addition to being inlaid with mosaics, were often filed on their biting surfaces into decorative points and zigzags, and bodies might be tattooed or painted.

Overleaf: Mayan ways still live—
Left: Transporting heavy burdens on human backs as in Mayan times
Right: Weaving a belt on the Mayan hip loom
(note leather backstrap on unused loom in foreground)

While most roads in the Guatemalan highlands were little more than foot trails, the Maya of the classic period built raised causeways of fitted limestone blocks through the jungle to facilitate trade. Rulers rode in litters carried by human bearers. But goods, no matter how heavy, were transported on men's backs in large wicker frames or net bags connected to a tumpline, or forehead strap. Women's burdens rode atop their heads. These patterns persist in the Indian sector of Guatemala to this day.

The homes of the Indian farmers have also changed very little over the centuries. In the hot lowlands, peasant huts were constructed of spaced cane poles lashed together with vines and had deeply pitched roofs covered with palm thatch. In cooler climates, walls of adobe, or sun-dried brick, were preferred, and a tall field grass (called *pajón* in Spanish and meaning "big straw") provided the thatch.

Clothing was woven of locally grown cotton on narrow backstrap, or hip, looms, like those the Maya still use today. One end of the loom was tied to a pole or tree while the other end was looped around the body of the weaver, who sat kneeling on the ground. Threads were colored with natural dyes. Blue was derived from the indigo plant, browns, rusts, and golds came from the logwood tree that grows in the Petén, and red was made from the dried body of the cochineal bug.

The simplest and most common garment of the lowland Maya was a straight, short kilt wrapped around the waist. Women sometimes wore a huipil (wee-PEEL), a short or medium-length shift with an opening for the neck, its sides left unsewn. The priests and other members of the ruling class dressed much more grandly in kilts of jaguar or ocelot skins or of cloth finely interwoven with hummingbird feathers. Headdresses were of colorful macaw or toucan feathers plucked from jungle birds. But most highly prized were the three-foot-long glinting, green-gold tail feathers of the quetzal, which came from the cloud-misted high-lands and were reserved for the most powerful rulers.

Religion was the center of Mayan life. Arts, crafts, music, the sciences, and even recreation revolved around the mythology of the gods and the rituals of worship. Religious ceremonies involved the burning of the incense copal, a semitransparent amber resin from a jungle-growing tree. Most of the gods represented nature—the sun, rain, sky, earth. Some took animal forms such as jaguars and serpents. There appears to have been a supreme deity named Itzamná and a moon goddess named Ixchel, who was probably his wife. She was also the patroness of fertility and childbirth.

Music accompanied religious rites and processions. The principal instruments, still played on the church steps of Indian villages today, were the *tun*, a drum made from a hollowed log or tree trunk, and the *chirimía*, a reed flute with sweet, silvery tones. There were also clay whistles, wooden horns, conch shells, and gourd rattles filled with seeds or beans. Some historians say that the Maya had a portable marimba fashioned out of elongated gourds strung together and tied around the waist. The player produced notes by tapping on the different-sized gourds with a pair of rubber-tipped sticks. But others argue that the modern marimba, which is Guatemala's national instrument, was transplanted from Africa.

In any case, the Maya did have rubber from various latex-producing tropical plants. They fashioned a hard bouncing ball for their ball game, which was played by two teams and was scored by striking the ball against certain marked areas along the walls of the rectangular court. In Mexico, some Indian ball courts had stone rings high up on their walls, presumably for the ball to pass through.

The players were forbidden to use their hands but could strike the ball with their hips and other parts of the body, as in soccer. The exact relation of the ball game to the Mayan religion is not known. But players purified themselves in the sweathouse beforehand, the priests blessed the playing ground, and the losing team often paid with its life, its members becoming sacrifices to the gods.

The stern dictates of the gods, which had given Tikal life, may well have brought about its decline. Possibly the demands of the priesthood for arduous temple building and extensive food production had become too great. Did the peasantry revolt against the cold, imperious ruler class? Was there insufficient access to the trade goods that were increasingly important to the complex society of Tikal?

Mayan scholars believe that those two factors were primarily responsible for the breakdown in Tikal's social structure. Was there also a prolonged drought, an epidemic, overpopulation, invasion, war? Perhaps some of these disasters, too, contributed to the abandonment of Tikal, as well as other great ceremonial centers of its day. In any case, the last stelae are dated in the late ninth century, and the year 900 is given as the close of the classic period. The peasant structures of cane and thatch quickly became one with the soil, and the jungle crept across the clearings entangling, uprooting, and eventually burying all but the tallest of the limestone temples that had been offered to the gods. Little was known of Tikal until nearly a thousand years later when the chicle gatherers of the Petén came across the ruins, opening the way for archeological investigation.

The drift of people from the Petén was both northward into Mexico and southward back to the highlands. Already during the

A ruler in quetzal feather headdress depicted on a stela at Tikal

46

classic period, starting in A.D. 600, the Maya had established magnificent ceremonial centers at Chichén Itzá and elsewhere on the Yucatán peninsula. But by the 900's, they were falling under the influence of the warriorlike Toltecs, who had swept down from central Mexico, and their culture was disintegrating.

The Maya who moved southward also bore traces of intermixture with Mexican Indian peoples. Back in the highlands they encountered other Mayan groups that had never left the area. The new population mix was more warlike and sought out defen-

A squat pyramid at the postclassic archeological site of Iximché

sible highland sites rather than sprawling plateaus like that on which Kaminaljuyú had been built.

The ceremonial cities of the postclassic period were less impressive than those of the lowlands. Squat pyramids supported temples with roofs of wood or thatch that rested on stone columns. The ruling class lived more austerely, and the common people devoted more of their time to agriculture and weaving. The imperial metropolis had faded and given way to a new order, that of a warrior and peasant society.

When the Spanish invader Pedro de Alvarado arrived, in 1524, the Indian nations of Guatemala were already divided. Using the strategy of allying his armies with one group to destroy another, and then turning on the first, he found conquest to be an easy matter. The land of the quetzal dropped into his hands almost as though it were intended as a gift from the Mayan gods.

11

Spanish Conquest and Culture

The Spanish conquerors reached Guatemala fresh from their victories in Mexico and the Caribbean. Their weapons were the sword and the cross, with which they had recently driven the Moors out of Spain in 1492. So not surprisingly their missionary zeal carried over into the New World. Firstly their approach was to overwhelm the inhabitants, by force if necessary, and secondly to convert them to Christianity.

The main object of Spain's campaign of conquest was to acquire tangible wealth: gold, silver, gems, ivory, silks, and spices, such as Columbus had hoped to find in the East Indies. Colonization by small farmers, artisans, and merchants—the pattern of settlement in New England and elsewhere in northern America—was never the goal of the conquistadors.

Unlike England, which had already developed a mercantile system that included small-scale farming and manufacturing, Spain was still a feudal society. As throughout the Middle Ages, its population was divided into two main groups: lords and vassals. In the New World, even the lowliest Spanish soldier proposed to become a lord; his vassals would be drawn from the Indian inhabitants of the newly conquered territory.

Spain's very first contact with the isthmus of Central America came as early as 1501, only nine years after Columbus first touched land in the western hemisphere. A Spanish ship under the command of Rodrigo de Bastidas, and carrying Vasco Núñez de Balboa, sailed into the Gulf of Darien near the present-day border between Panama and Colombia. In 1513, Balboa, who had returned to the region, marched across the isthmus, gained his first view of the Pacific, and claimed all the lands along its shores for Spain.

Costa Rica and Nicaragua were subsequently penetrated by expeditions heading north from Panama. Guatemala, El Salvador, and Honduras, however, were taken by Spaniards coming south from Mexico. Hernán Cortés invaded Mexico in 1519 and was eager for further exploration. Late in 1523 Pedro de Alvarado, Cortés' second-in-command, set out for the lands that lay to the south, and by the early part of 1524 he had completed the difficult overland journey from Mexico City to Guatemala.

Alvarado was accompanied by several hundred Spanish soldiers, more than a hundred horses, and many thousands of Mexican Indian warriors. Most were Tlaxcaltecs, neighbors of the Aztecs who had allied themselves with the Spanish to defeat their Aztec enemies. Probably the Tlaxcaltecs were the ones who bestowed the name Guatemala, a Mexican Indian word meaning "land of forests" or "place of trees," on the newly invaded territory.

By this time, the Maya-Quiché had emerged as the most powerful of the highland peoples, and Alvarado entered into battle with them. Aided by local allies, he faced the Quiché chieftain Tecún Umán in hand-to-hand combat. According to Mayan legend, Tecún was accompanied during the struggle by a quetzal bird, which always flew beside him when he fought his enemies. The quetzal is said to have been Tecún's nagual, or animal cospirit. Mayans to this day believe that each person has a protective animal counterpart that will be revealed through a mystical ex-

perience during one's lifetime. One must never harm one's nagual, even unintentionally.

Supposedly, in the struggle between Tecún and Alvarado, Tecún perceived the horse on which Alvarado was mounted to be *his* animal cospirit. Therefore, when Tecún struck at the horse's neck drawing blood, he believed that he had killed Alvarado. But Alvarado, unharmed, slashed at Tecún with his sword and wounded him mortally. At that moment, according to legend, the quetzal bird, which had formerly been green all over, was splashed with Tecún's blood and received the bright crimson breast that it wears to this day.

Historically, Tecún Umán's death marked the defeat of the Indians of Guatemala by the Spanish, just as the death of Montezuma, the Aztec king, had signaled the subjugation of all of Mexico. The remnants of the Quiché fought desperately, but their stone-tipped spears and tapir-skin shields were no match for the forged-steel weapons and explosive firearms of the Spaniards. Also the psychological advantage of the Spanish horsemen was enormous. The Indians had never before seen horses and so attributed mystical properties to them. Many believed, like the Quiché chieftain, that the horse and rider were spiritually one, a supernatural being.

On July 25, 1524, the day of Santiago Apóstol (St. James the Apostle, the patron saint of Spain), Alvarado founded his capital at the present-day town of Tecpán on a high plateau near Iximché, a fortresslike Mayan ceremonial center. The city was named Santiago de los Caballeros de Guatemala. Significantly the word *caballero* means horseman as well as knight or nobleman.

Other Indian peoples of the highlands and the Pacific region

Tecún Umán, the defeated Quiché chieftain

were subdued, and in 1527 Alvarado moved his capital to a more accessible site near the base of the volcano Agua. Today the second colonial capital is known as Ciudad Vieja, or Old City.

However, Alvarado was not happy as governor of Guatemala, for the new domain failed to produce any precious metals. Making forays· into neighboring territory, he discovered that Honduras had some streams containing particles and even small nuggets of gold, but the yield turned out to be limited. Leaving the governorship to his lieutenants for long periods of time, Alvarado began to explore other sites, visited Spain, and finally was killed fighting the Indians in Mexico. He died at Guadalajara in 1541.

Two months after Alvarado's death, the second colonial capital was destroyed by the earth tremors that unleashed the watery contents of Agua's crater. Alvarado's widow, Beatriz de la Cueva, who had assumed the governorship, was among those killed in the disaster.

A third capital had to be built, and it was founded a couple of years later just a few miles away from Ciudad Vieja. The name conferred on the new city was La muy Noble y la muy Leal Ciudad de Santiago de los Caballeros de Guatemala, The most Noble and most Loyal City of St. James of the Knights of Guatemala. Today this city is known as Antigua Guatemala, or simply Antigua.

The new Santiago was grandly laid out in traditional Spanish style, with a long, two-story colonnaded administration palace

Left: Pedro de Alvarado, the Spanish conqueror of Guatemala
Overleaf: Scenes of two capital cities—
Left: The church in Ciudad Vieja,
the second colonial capital that was destroyed in 1541
Right: The volcano Agua, viewed through the Arch of Santa Catalina in Antigua

The cloister of the Convent of the Capuchines in Antigua

and a great cathedral flanking the spacious main plaza. Churches, monasteries, cloistered convents, and the mansions of the wealthy were built all around the city. Santiago was not merely the capital of Guatemala, for in 1543 the Spanish crown named it the seat of government of a vast domain that included Chiapas (now a state of Mexico) and ranged all the way to the Panamanian border.

Within the boundaries of the new "kingdom," or Captaincy-General, of Guatemala lay the territories of Belize, El Salvador, Honduras, Nicaragua, and Costa Rica, many parts of which had never been officially secured or even explored by the Spanish. Nevertheless, the region was often referred to as the Kingdom of Guatemala, and the status of the captains-general who adminis-tered it was only a notch or two lower than that of the two vice-

58

roys who, in the name of the king of Spain, governed Mexico and Peru. Panama was included in the Viceroyalty of Peru, which was headquartered in Lima.

During the seventeenth century, Santiago's population grew to around 60,000. Although smaller than either Mexico City or Lima, it ranked with them as one of the three most important and affluent cities in the New World. Santiago was also a center of learning and law. One of the first printing presses in the Americas was installed there in 1660. Although used mainly to disseminate religious works, secular materials including a newspaper were also produced after a time. In 1681, the first Guatemalan university, San Carlos de Borromeo, was founded. The Spanish *audiencia*, or supreme court of justice for the entire Captaincy-General, sat in Santiago.

The authority vested in its capital did not, however, give the

The University of San Carlos de Borromeo, now the Colonial Museum

The fortress of San Felipe de Lara, built to repel English buccaneers

Kingdom of Guatemala complete control over its territory. English pirates and smugglers, who had begun raiding Spain's possessions in the Caribbean in the 1600's, also infiltrated the shores of Honduras and Nicaragua. This area, named for the indigenous Mosquito Indians, was known as the Mosquito Coast. Closer to the Guatemalan heartland, English loggers established a toehold at the mouth of the Belize River, where they began cutting the valuable dyewoods and mahogany that grew all across the jungles of Belize and the Petén.

A more direct threat to the capital came from English buccaneers who sailed up the Río Dulce into Lake Izabal. To repel their attacks on shipments of cacao and indigo bound for Spain, the Spanish built the fortress of San Felipe de Lara at the point where Lake Izabal feeds into the river. Upon its completion, in

1652, they stretched a mighty chain across the river to prevent passage into the lake.

While the British gradually backed off in most parts of Central America, their claim to Belize (also known as British Honduras) as a colonial possession dates from the early days of the logging trade. The word Belize, incidentally, is believed to be a corruption of the name of the seventeenth-century English buccaneer Peter Wallace. As a black Caribbean laboring population filtered into the English-speaking colony, other changes in pronunciation and spelling took place. The coastal town of Stann Creek, for example, was originally called St. Ann's Creek by the English settlers.

During the first decades of Spanish colonization, few African slaves were brought to Central America, for the Indians provided a ready-made labor force. From their experiences in the Caribbean, where many Indians had died off, some of the Spanish administrators had learned the value of preserving the local population, to work in the mines, at agriculture, or in whatever enterprise provided the best means of extracting riches from the colony.

In Panama, Nicaragua, and Honduras, however, the Indians were so harshly treated that many again began to die off. In addition, European epidemic diseases like smallpox, measles, and typhus took a heavy toll. On the newly established coastal plantations, the Indian slaves suffered the ravages of malaria and yellow fever.

By 1542, when the Spanish crown issued an order outlawing Indian slavery, the inhabitants of Panama had already been decimated. As a result, blacks were imported to work as mule drivers and canoemen in the steaming swamps and jungles. Panama was the transisthmian route over which the gold and silver of Peru, Spain's richest find in the Americas, was carried. The treasure was then loaded onto ships bound for the mother country.

In Nicaragua and Honduras, the eventual dying off of the Indians brought black slaves to work on the sugar plantations and in the Honduran silver mines discovered at Tegucigalpa in 1569. Costa Rica, unlike its neighbors, had no major exports and few Indians or blacks to exploit in the early years of colonization. Much later, during the 1800's, coffee growing was introduced. But the cultivation of this crop became the province of small-scale European farmers. This development helps to explain why countries like Panama, Nicaragua, and Honduras today have racially mixed populations, while Costa Rica has a predominantly white population and also a much more egalitarian social structure.

Guatemala and, to a lesser extent, El Salvador had the largest concentration of Indians. The Guatemalan highlands, in particular, were made up of settled Mayan agriculturalists living in small communities and following their deep-rooted traditions.

Rebellions against the Spanish were not uncommon. Often they bribed the Indian leaders to help them maintain control. If the leaders refused to cooperate, they themselves might be taken hostage as a means of persuasion. Particularly fierce in their opposition to the conquerors were the Kekchí and Pokomchí nations of the regions to the north of the capital known as the Land of War. Finally, through the efforts of Bartolomé de las Casas, the missionary priest who had worked with the Indians in the Caribbean and Mexico, the inhabitants were converted to Christianity and to a more peaceable attitude toward the Spanish. Las Casas, who began his campaign in 1537, is considered responsible for turning the Land of War into the Land of True Peace, today designated as the departments of Alta (Upper) and Baja (Lower) Verapaz, or True Peace.

A mural in the museum in San Pedro Carchá depicting Bartolomé de las Casas (left) among the Indians in the Land of War

The Indians' violent objections to the Spanish overlords were well-founded. Greedy landowners not only appropriated the best Indian lands, they devised forced-labor systems that barely skirted the Indian-slavery ban of 1542 and denied the Indians any true freedom.

The two systems introduced were the *encomienda* and the *repartimiento*. The *encomienda* was a holdover from feudal Europe, under which the peasants of a particular region "commended" themselves to a lord for military protection. In exchange, they lived and toiled on his estate. In the New World, the *encomendero*, or *patrón*, was supposed to see to the peasants' general welfare and religious education in return for their serfdom. The *encomienda* worked a special hardship in Guatemala because Indian families had to leave their own land, to which they were deeply devoted, and move to the land of the *patrón*.

The *repartimiento,* which was introduced about 1550, was a work-levy system requiring men between the ages of sixteen and sixty to donate several days of labor each week to individual landowners, the church, or the Government. Often the Indians had to make long journeys on foot, neglecting their own farms. Indian conscript laborers were not always paid for their work, and frequently their pittances vanished into the payment of debts for items consumed on the job or into special taxes levied on them.

The Indians were clearly at the bottom of the social and economic scale in colonial society, which was sharply stratified into classes. At the top were the Spanish-born officials, clergy, and landowners, known as *peninsulares* (born on the Iberian peninsula). Of somewhat lower status, but still ranking high in the society, were the *criollos,* or Creoles. They were also of pure Spanish blood, but had been born in Central America.

A third group, of considerably lower prestige, was made up of individuals of mixed parentage, usually a Spanish father and an Indian mother. They were known as mestizos, a term still used for racially mixed persons in Nicaragua and Panama and also in Mexico. In Guatemala, El Salvador, and Honduras, however, the word Ladino gradually came into use. While mestizo is strictly a racial designation, Ladino—meaning a Latinized Indian or other person—has a broad cultural application. In Guatemala, a person who is of pure Indian blood but does not live an Indian way of life may be called a Ladino. At the same time, the word Ladino may be applied to a pure-blooded *criollo.*

During the early colonial period in Central America, the offspring of Indians and blacks were known as zambos. Today the descendants of black slaves have been absorbed into the Ladino or mestizo groups. People of African ancestry range from very few in Guatemala to considerably more in Nicaragua and Panama.

Little effort was made to preserve the rich culture of the *naturales*, or *indígenas*, as the Indians of Guatemala are today known. The Spanish tendency was to impose its language, religion, laws, agriculture, economy, and political system on its conquered peoples, and the Spanish clergy was particularly vehement in denouncing the Mayan religious beliefs as superstitious falsehoods. Many of the Mayan books in the form of codices, or manuscripts, in which hieroglyphs were inscribed in color on paper made from pounded bark, were burned.

There were, however, a few exceptions to this destruction of the written records of the Maya. Shortly after the conquest, the Quiché managed to produce the *Popol Vuh*, which tells of their history, religion, and mythology. This sacred book was written in the Quiché language using the Roman alphabet. A similar text, which tells of the ruling dynasties of another important Mayan nation, is the *Annals of the Cakchiquels*.

Further information about the Maya was preserved by Diego de Landa, a Spanish bishop of the Yucatán who arrived there in 1549. Although de Landa tried to stamp out the religious practices of the Maya, he also recorded many details about the workings of their calendar and opened the way to the deciphering of their glyphs.

Despite the wide gulf that appeared to separate the Mayan religious beliefs from Christianity, there were a number of similarities between them. The Mayans had many gods, the Christians had many saints. Both religions revolved around a belief in the afterlife, with concepts of heaven and hell. Both involved elaborate rituals and ceremonial processions. Even the symbol

of the cross was not unfamiliar to the Mayans, who had devised such a form to represent the four winds of heaven.

The blending of the two religions is seen today in many of Guatemala's Indian villages, where churches are decorated with effigies of Christian saints and Mayan gods side by side. In Chichicastenango, in the department of Quiché, the Indians of the surrounding area converge every Thursday and Sunday to hold a market and to worship at the Church of Santo Tomás. The first homage to the saints or gods is made before a fire burning brightly on the stone steps of the church. Next the supplicant may swing a perforated can of burning incense on the upper steps near the entrance. It is believed that the smoke will send one's prayers to heaven.

Inside the church, the faithful kneel at shrines set out in

Left: Mayan hieroglyphs, squares of picture writing,
carved on a stela at Quiriguá
Below: Christian saints and a Mayan god in the church
at Santiago Atitlán

Above: Paying homage before the fire on the steps
of the Church of Santo Tomás in Chichicastenango
Right: The Basilica of Esquipulas, which houses the Black Christ

squares on the floor. There they burn candles and scatter ever-
green needles and the petals of marigolds and other flowers that
symbolize health, money, friendship, love, inner tranquility, and
other desires of their prayers. The sprinkling of the shrine with
aguardiente, a fiery rum distilled from sugarcane, seems to be
a final act of sanctification as the god-saints are beseeched or
perhaps railed against for not having answered earlier prayers.

Although the Spanish colonial clergy looked with disfavor
on the Indian interpretation of Christianity, they learned to ac-
commodate to it. In fact, they encouraged the sculptor Quirio
Cataño to carve a figure of Christ out of dark wood, presumably

to achieve identification with the dark-skinned Indians. The five-foot statue, completed in 1594, was placed in a chapel at Esquipulas, in eastern Guatemala, where an Indian convert was said to have had a vision of Jesus. Later, in 1758, an imposing white basilica in colonial "wedding-cake" style was built to house the Black Christ.

While Christianity found varying degrees of acceptance among the Indians of Guatemala, the Spanish language was rejected by a large proportion of the inhabitants. Mayan tongues are still spoken by perhaps 40 percent of the 7.2 million Guatemalans—possibly 3 million people—for they best express both the abstract ideas and the everyday needs of this large group that still follows an Indian way of life. Most Indians do learn some Spanish, of course, to use in their dealings in the marketplace and in their relatively infrequent contacts with the civil authorities. And, as might be expected, certain Indian words have taken a permanent place in Guatemalan Spanish. Among them are huipil, for a woman's blouse rather than the Spanish *blusa*; milpa, for corn-field; and many place names.

The Indians did, however, adopt a number of features of Spanish dress at the time of the conquest. Having abandoned the Mayan kilt, the men of Chichicastenango, for example, took as their habitual garb a version of the Spanish officers' outfit of the sixteenth century. It consisted of a short, stiff jacket and knee-length breeches of black undyed wool, richly embroidered or appliqued in bright colors. Wool, of course, was unknown in Central America until the introduction of sheep from Spain.

The men of other Indian villages adopted Spanish-style *camisas*, or shirts, and *pantalones*, which varied from knee-length to ankle-length. In the village of Santiago Atitlán, on the shore of Lake Atitlán, purple-and-white-striped knee-length trousers are worn to this day.

70

Women's clothing was altered, too, in response to the Spanish demand for modesty. The loose huipil of varying length became a blouse worn with a wrapped skirt that was given the Spanish name of *corte* (KOR-teh), meaning a length of cloth. The skirt was held up at the waist with the Spanish *faja* (FAH-hah), or sash.

Headdresses were a holdover from the preconquest era. Both

The Spanish-inspired garb worn by the men of Chichicastenango

men and women wore and still wear the practical Mayan *tzute* (ZUH-teh), or headcloth, which can serve strictly as headgear or be unfolded to provide a carrying cloth or baby sling. In some villages, the women braid brightly colored wool or ribbons into their hair as a form of headdress.

Although many Indians continue to go barefoot, some have adopted sandals. One of the cheapest modern kinds is cut from old rubber tires. A friendly nickname for the *guatemalteco* or *guatemalteca* (Guatemalan man or woman) is *chapín* or *chapina*. The *chapín* was actually a cork-soled Spanish clog, adapted to colonial use. Today the nickname is simply a familiar tag for a Guatemalan, identifying him or her as the supposed wearer of some sort of informal footgear.

Hides for leather, tallow for soap and candles, and, of course, meat, milk, and cheese were by-products of the cattle that the Spanish introduced into the New World. The hogs brought by the Spanish provided pork and lard, or hog fat, for frying, while chickens were a new source of poultry and eggs in addition to the domesticated turkeys that the Indians already raised.

The introduction of livestock also revolutionized transportation in Central America. Now there was the horse for the Spanish landowner or officer to ride, the donkey or burro to serve as a pack animal, and the mule and the ox for drayage. Along with draft animals, came the *carreta*, the Spanish two-wheeled cart of Mediterranean origin, the first wheeled vehicle.

Yet the highland Indian resisted the new means of transportation, continuing to carry most articles on his back. His motives were practical. The mountains in which he lived and labored were threaded with footpaths too narrow and rugged to permit

A woman wearing a huipil with a skirt adapted from the Spanish

the passage of wheels. Pack animals might have served, but they were costly to buy and feed. As to horses and even mules, only the Spanish and the highest-ranking Indians, such as village chiefs or mayors, were permitted to mount these beasts.

Spanish stock raising claimed large tracts of land, often appropriated from the Indians, for the newly introduced animals throve best in the western highlands. The cattle, horses, and mules of the Spaniards also made demands on the domestic food supply. The sheep and goats overgrazed the hillsides and caused soil erosion. Nevertheless, the haciendas, or ranches, steadily expanded their holdings. Each was a self-contained unit, almost a walled village. In addition to its main house and workers' huts, its corrals, croplands, and granaries, each had its own workshops, its own *tienda,* or general store, and its own priest and chapel.

The less prosperous Spanish colonials settled on the drier lands of Oriente to farm and raise cattle. Many of the Indians of that region, descendants of the Mayans who had once worshipped at Quiriguá and at Copán in nearby Honduras, resisted the Spanish and were massacred. The remainder soon integrated with the settler population and lost their Indian identity. As a result, Oriente today is distinctly Ladino. The farmers still grow corn and eat tortillas, but they use European farm tools and ox-drawn plows instead of the Indian dibble. Their adobe-walled houses are generally roofed with Spanish-style tiles rather than thatch, and they use the *carreta* for transportation. The men wear wide-brimmed straw hats against the sun, ride horseback, usually carry guns, and are fiercely imbued with male pride in matters of honor and community standing. In fact, this region so closely resembles the old-time American "wild west" that Oriente has been called the "wild east" of Guatemala.

Although the Spanish introduced many new food crops to the Americas, Indian corn remained the staple of Guatemala, for it

In the highlands of Chimaltenango—
a newly harvested crop of corn, Guatemala's staple food

grew better than wheat in most parts of the country. Also its place was firmly fixed in Indian mythology. The *Popol Vuh* relates that the creator first tried to fashion man out of clay, but this substance proved too fragile. He then tried wood, but it was too rigid. Lastly he made four men of corn paste, or masa, the very same doughy mass of crushed, hulled kernels from which tortillas are fashioned. The men lived and were given wives of corn paste, and so the human race was created.

The foods of the conquerors blended, however, with the corn, beans, squash, tomatoes, avocados, and chili peppers of the Indians and expanded the variety of dishes and their flavors. Lentils and chick peas joined the black beans of Guatemala, although

75

black beans still hold a central place in the national cuisine. Onions and garlic were combined with chili seasoning to add piquancy to tortilla fillings and to the mashed avocado mixture known as guacamole.

Most of the new vegetables grew best in the *tierra templada*, as did Mediterranean fruits like the apple, peach, quince, fig, and pomegranate. Oddly, grapevines and olive trees, so extensively cultivated in Spain, were not widely grown in Spanish colonial America. The reason was primarily economic. Spain forbade the colonies to produce wine or oil commercially, decreeing that these products should be imported from the mother country.

Sugarcane, bananas, plantains (the *plátano*, or cooking banana), rice, mangoes, and citrus fruits, although brought to the New World by the Spanish, were actually of Asian origin and most accommodated well to the *tierra caliente*, the tropical lowlands. Sugar became an export crop while locally sugarcane juice, highly distilled, provided a new alcoholic beverage, *aguardiente de caña*. Formerly, the fermented beverages of the Indians had been made from corn and from various fruits.

The cultivation of cacao, which had been grown from early times by the Maya, was taken over and expanded by Spanish plantation owners. The Indians, lacking sugar, had pulverized the dark brown beans and mixed them with dried chili peppers and various herbs, using the blend as a seasoning. But the Spanish combined the chocolate derived from the beans with sugar and concocted a rich beverage that came into great demand in the colonies and in Spain as well. Just as cacao beans had probably been used as currency at times during the classic and postclassic

The banana, introduced by the Spanish,
which grows lushly in Guatemala's tropical lowlands

Mayan periods, they were sometimes used to pay Indian laborers in the 1500's. The number of beans equivalent to a Spanish silver peso fluctuated, depending on the scarcity or abundance of the crop.

Many indigenous nonfood crops became profitable exports. Among the most valued were dyes for the textile mills of northwestern Europe, especially indigo, the leaves of which yielded a deep blue coloring. The indigo plant had long grown wild in the Pacific region of Central America. Now the Spanish landowners established plantations in the coastal lowlands of Guatemala, El Salvador, Honduras, and Nicaragua. To extract the dye from the plants, the leaves were put into stone vats and converted into a pasty residue. The residue was then dried and cut into bars for shipment abroad. Most of the region's indigo processing was done by African slaves. Trade was brisk from 1550 to around 1850. Then the development of aniline, or coal-tar, dyes in Europe signaled a sharply declining demand for the natural product.

Another dye that was important in the colonial economy was cochineal, prized for its rich scarlet color. Cochineal was extracted from the dried bodies of a species of tiny scale insect that throve on the leaves of the nopal, or prickly pear, cactus. The preconquest Maya had developed nopalries—adobe-walled enclosures of nopal plants where cochineal bugs could be raised protected from wind and from insect-eating animals—and they continued this industry under Spanish supervision. Like indigo, cochineal lost its market soon after synthetic dyes came on the scene.

Tobacco, cotton, and maguey were other exports of the Kingdom of Guatemala. The maguey cactus was a fiber-yielding plant from which rope and cordage products were manufactured by the Indians.

Hand-woven textiles and other crafted goods were important in the domestic economy of Guatemala, as was leather working. To keep up with the foreign demand for hides and other cattle products, the prosperous Spanish hacendados gradually moved their ranches from the highlands to the more spacious Pacific coastal plain where the cattle-raising industry thrives today. At first, the animals suffered from parasitic ticks and cattle diseases, rampant in the tropical lowlands. But these problems were eventually overcome through crossbreeding with more resistant stock.

Despite its roster of exports, the economy of Central America remained relatively stagnant during the colonial era. Growth was held back by a number of factors. Spain restricted trade among the colonies and also with foreign powers other than the mother country. The forbidding terrain meant that roads were few and communications were poor. Guatemala's chief Caribbean port, Santo Tomás de Castilla, never attained the shipping volume of Veracruz on the Gulf Coast of Mexico.

A great blow to the Captaincy-General was struck in 1773 when the capital of Santiago was rocked by a series of massive earthquakes. Cathedrals and Government buildings toppled; convents, monasteries, the mansions of the rich, and the hovels of the poor came crashing down on their occupants. Water and food became scarce, and disease broke out. Most of the city, the richest expression of Spanish colonial architecture, lay in ruins.

Although the clergy was reluctant to abandon the city with its dozens of churches, the civil authorities set about choosing a new site for the capital about thirty miles to the east in the valley of La Ermita. In 1776, New Guatemala of the Assumption—today known as Guatemala City—was founded. Santiago, the former capital, began to be referred to as Antigua, or Old, Guatemala. Today this handsome, museumlike, colonial city is preserved as a national monument by Government decree.

Antigua's restored La Merced Church,
which suffered only minor damage in the 1773 earthquake

The late 1700's were also a time of political upheaval in the
Western world. Revolutions took place in North America's Thir-
teen Colonies and in royalist France. In Central America, the
colonial Government was now in the hands of the Creoles, whose
first loyalty was to their birthplace rather than to Spain. Resentment against the mother country's political, economic, and religious domination was growing. Sentiments for independence were
voiced, and proindependence writings began to be published in
the capital.

For Central America, independence from Spain came blood-
lessly on September 15, 1821, after Mexico won its independence. The main concern of the Captaincy-General was whether
to permit itself to become part of Mexico or to fight for a separate independence. There was a brief, unsatisfactory period of

annexation with Mexico, but on July 1, 1823 the Central American states declared themselves wholly independent. Known as the United Provinces of Central America, they consisted of Guatemala, El Salvador, Honduras, Nicaragua, and Costa Rica. Chiapas had elected to remain part of Mexico, becoming one of that country's thirty-one states.

Although their transition to independence had been peaceful, there were growing problems of disunity within the United Provinces of Central America. There were also distinct racial differences. On the eve of independence, the composition of the Captaincy-General was 65 percent Indian, 31 percent mestizo, and 4 percent Creole and Spanish. Yet these averages were not typical for any one province. Guatemala and Chiapas had many more Indians than the average, while El Salvador and Honduras had fewer. Nicaragua had the largest racially mixed population, about 84 percent mestizo, while Costa Rica was mainly European.

But the trend toward individual autonomy within the United Provinces was not based on racial variations alone. The remoteness of Guatemala City from the provincial capitals, the scattered population clusters of the isthmus, the difficulties of transportation and communication had helped give rise to local leaders who challenged the authority of the capital. Also, there were varying philosophies of government within the provinces. Once independence was achieved, they divided into two main political camps: Conservative and Liberal.

The Conservatives were traditionalists. Their ideas of government were rooted in the colonial past. They supported the power of the church, which under Spanish rule had been a major landowner, had the right to impose taxes on the public, had completely controlled education, and was the only institution that could sanction marriage. The Conservatives also supported the old Spanish judicial system with its often harsh judgments and denial of rights of appeal.

The ideas of the Liberals were derived in part from those of England, postrevolutionary France, and the young United States. They wanted to check the power of the church and to institute public education, civil marriage, trial by jury, and other social and legal reforms. Each of the United Provinces had both Liberal and Conservative elements battling for control, with one or the other gaining the upper hand at different times so that the provinces were seldom in full agreement. These conflicts bred political rivalry and opportunism.

The philosophy of the Liberals, unfortunately, did not include ideas of social equality or equal economic opportunity for the Indians, the coastal-dwelling blacks, or the racially mixed peo-

Guatemala City's Plazuela España, which featured a statue of the king of Spain that was destroyed at the time of independence

ples of the isthmus. Although slavery was prohibited in the United Provinces, the Indians and other non-Europeans were still viewed as chattels. Their labor was essential to the economic system, and the privileged class was thought to have a right to exploit it, using the *repartimiento,* debt peonage, or other forced-work systems if necessary.

Thus, forms of government that were absolutist and dictatorial rather than democratic developed in Central America. The single exception was Costa Rica, where the few Indians had been exterminated in the early years of Spanish conquest and the white-settler farming population that took over tended to establish a democratic political tradition.

In 1815, Simón Bolívar, the South American revolutionist who liberated much of the continent from Spain, wrote the following hopeful words about Central America:

The States of the Isthmus from Panama to Guatemala will perhaps form a confederation. This magnificent location between the two great oceans could in time become the emporium of the world. Its canals will shorten the distances throughout the world, strengthen commercial ties with Europe, America, and Asia, and bring that happy region tribute from the four quarters of the globe. Perhaps some day the capital of the world may be located there, just as Constantine claimed Byzantium was the capital of the ancient world.

Bolívar's prophecy was fulfilled only in part. A canal would be built, but the isthmus would not become the capital of the world. There would be marked economic development, but the permanent political confederation of which Bolívar dreamed would be shattered within fifteen years of the formation of the United Provinces of Central America.

The years 1837 and 1838 saw both a cholera epidemic and a popular uprising in Central America. The two were related, for the ravages of widespread disease fueled discontent with the Government under Liberal leader Mariano Gálvez.

Gálvez, true to the Liberal philosophy, had curbed the church, introduced secular education, and instituted the Livingston Code. This legal system, set forth by a Louisiana jurist, guaranteed trial by jury and other enlightened judicial practices.

However, in spite of his well-meant reforms, Gálvez was authoritarian in his methods. He had aroused enmity in the general public and was strongly opposed by the upper class Conservatives. The states' righters in the provinces, who had long been agitating for more autonomy, took the opportunity to break free in 1838. In the course of the politically chaotic events surrounding Gálvez, the provinces cast off the domination of Guatemala City and declared themselves sovereign and independent republics.

Stripped of El Salvador, Honduras, Nicaragua, and Costa Rica, Guatemala stood alone, a predominantly Indian nation in which Spanish conquest had succeeded but Spanish culture had not penetrated as deeply as elsewhere in Middle America. The obstacle in Guatemala was not only the high proportion of pure-blooded Indians but their Mayan nationhood. Despite the many Hispanic influences at work, their Indian ways prevailed so strongly that to the present day they constitute a society within a society—a living remnant of the past.

The distinct contrast between Guatemala's Indian and Ladino ways of life makes that country unique among modern Hispano-American nations. However, while providing a rich cultural ferment, that condition has also compounded Guatemala's social and economic problems.

III

Living in Guatemala Today

In Guatemala City, the story is told about an Indian recently transplanted from the western highlands who became the caretaker of a new multistory office building. Within six months, tall foliage crackling in the wind was observed on its roof. A closer look revealed a thriving patch of corn, its heavy ears almost ready for harvesting.

Laboriously the Indian caretaker had carted baskets of earth from his home fields, planted the seed, and watered and weeded his token crop. In the Mayan belief, corn is the sustenance and, in fact, the very essence of human life. No matter where one lives, one must nurture the corn plant.

Although some city-born and -bred Ladinos were amused, most were not surprised by the caretaker's compulsion to grow corn twenty stories above the ground. The Indian of Guatemala is a remarkable combination of aloofness and adaptiveness, preserving the past while living in the present.

What is life really like among the Indians of Guatemala and how is it changing in response to pressures from the rest of the country and the world outside?

The size of Guatemala's Indian population can be estimated only roughly. The figures available do not reflect "door-to-door" counts or accurate record keeping, since none exists. It is believed, however, that racially Guatemala is at least 60 percent pure-blooded Indian, while culturally it is only about 43 percent Indian. In other words, this means that over 40 percent of all *indígenas,* or *naturales,* retain their ancestral identity, while perhaps 17 to 20 percent have passed over in some degree into the Ladino way of life.

Becoming a Ladino generally means leaving the family unit, discarding Indian dress, language, work patterns, and religious practices. It means giving up the dependence on hand-crafted products and entering a consumer society that relies primarily on mass-produced goods. It means participating in the nation's social, economic, and political mainstream.

The Indian is not barred from making this transition on racial grounds, for the Ladino sector is a racial cross section that ranges from Mayan to European. More likely the Indian is held back by lack of education and by lack of a job that provides self-sufficiency.

Nearly three-quarters of Guatemala's *indígenas* live in the highlands to the north and west of the capital, in eight of the country's twenty-two departments. Villages are laid out in the Spanish colonial pattern, not unlike that of the Mayan ceremonial sites, in which a central square is dominated by a religious structure. Since the conquest, of course, that structure has become a church rather than a pyramid-supported temple. Other sides of the plaza may be lined with the *alcaldía,* or city hall, possibly a telegraph office, a health clinic, and a school. The plaza itself, which may have a village well or fountain in the center, often serves as the central marketplace.

Streets lead out from the square. But on nonmarket days the Indian villages—like Chichicastenango and others—may appear deserted, for much of their population actually lives in the sur-

A street leading out of Chichicastenango to the rural hinterland,
where most of the township's population lives

rounding hills and valleys. Thus, the typical *municipio*, or township, includes a rural hinterland of tiny scattered hamlets in addition to the village center.

Indian houses are of rough, brown adobe brick, only occasionally plastered and seldom painted. As is true of modest Ladino
dwellings in certain parts of the country, roofs are of locally
gathered thatch, sometimes corrugated tin, and fences are of
dried cornstalks or rough poles. Inside there are generally one or
two rooms with earthen floors, no water or electricity, a crude
table and benches, mats or hammocks for sleeping, and a cooking hearth of raised earth or a few stones. There is seldom any
provision for ventilation other than the entryway, and the air in
close-packed communities hangs thick with the smoke of wood
and charcoal fires.

Some Indian homes have an adjoining *temaxcal*, or sweat bath, a holdover from the Mayan past that is used for ritual purification and cleansing. The *temaxcal* is a low-roofed stone hut, in which piles of rocks are heated and then dashed with water to produce steam.

Of Guatemala's entire population, 62 percent is rural so not surprisingly the country's Indians are primarily farmers. Corn, beans, and squash are still their principal crops and the mainstay of their diet. But a visit to an Indian marketplace reveals that a great variety of vegetables, grains, and fruits, including tubers, greens, herbs, seeds, and spices, are also eaten. Many of these items are grown mainly as cash crops. Dried fish from the lakes and rivers are displayed for sale, and live chickens and pigs are everywhere.

The basic Indian diet of tortillas, corn gruels, or corn-paste tamales eaten with beans was once thought to be inadequate in protein. But nutritionists have now discovered that corn and beans eaten together provide a high-quality protein that ranks with that of meat and eggs. The Maya of the past developed such a healthful natural diet, which did not require meat more than once a week, if that often. Many of today's Indians only suffer from malnutrition when they leave the community and take on Ladino eating patterns, substituting white bread for tortillas and adding quantities of refined sugar in the form of soft drinks and other junk foods. Indian sweets are usually made with "black" sugar, which is rich in minerals because of its high molasses content.

The main problem affecting the Indian farmer is lack of

Above: The courtyard of a group of Indian dwellings in Santiago Atitlán
Below: A thatch-roofed Ladino house in the town of Flores in the Petén

89

Above: Farmlands that have been terraced
to help make steep hillsides fruitful
Right: A variety of vegetables offered for sale
at the Indian market in the town of Patzicía

sufficient land on which to grow the food for his family's subsistence plus some to sell for cash income. Most highland plots are small, perhaps two to ten acres, and some are communal farmlands. The steepest hillsides are carefully terraced to get the maximum benefit from each holding as there has been no significant increase in the limited share of land allotted to the Indian at the time of the conquest. At the same time, plots are divided and subdivided as each generation of sons comes into its inheritance. Also, soils become exhausted and often must be left fallow for a number of years.

Cottage industries provide some additional income for the Indian. Using the Mayan backstrap loom, women weave many

Left: Selling blocks and rounds of "black" sugar,
some wrapped in straw, at an Indian marketplace
Above: Rolling corn masa on the stone metate,
and baking tortillas on the comal, or griddle

types of textile products for sale. They also weave everyday garments for themselves and their families in the distinctive colors and design motifs that are traditional for their particular village. Over a hundred different communities in present-day Guatemala can be identified by the clothing of their inhabitants.

Other home-crafted items taken to the markets are wool blankets, baskets, netting, reed mats, ceramics, and leather goods. At the Indian market, prices are not fixed and bargaining is the custom. Market days also serve a social function and, since the church is usually located directly on the market plaza, as an occasion for religious worship.

93

A display of colorful dyed fibers for use in home weaving

An important religious institution that has grown out of the Indian adoption of Christianity is the *cofradía*, or religious brotherhood. The *cofradía* began as a church-affiliated organization, or society, encouraged by the priests of the colonial era. The purpose of the brotherhood, which includes the most respected male members of the community, and often their wives, is to devote itself to the care and worship of a particular saint. Membership is usually for one year, and during that period the saint's statue is taken from the church and kept in the home of the head of the *cofradía*. On holy days, it is marched to the church in an elaborate procession.

To be the head of a *cofradía* confers the highest status, for the values of the Indian community are not based on wealth but on how strongly one upholds the traditions and contributes to communal life. *Cofradías* are fewer and less important among the Ladino population.

The fiesta of Santo Tomás, which takes place on December 21 at the church of the same name in Chichicastenango, brings forth the Indian *cofradías* of three saints. At that time, the images of St. Joseph and St. Sebastian, as well as St. Thomas, are carried to the accompaniment of fireworks and ritual dances.

A non-Christian feature of this celebration is the *palo volador*, or flying pole dance. Two intrepid fliers climb a tall pole erected in front of the church, bind themselves to long ropes connected to the top of the pole, and, making wide revolutions, gradually whirl to the ground. Their feat is accompanied by musicians playing the Mayan drum and flute and also the gourd marimba. The *palo volador*, which is similar to a Mexican version with four fliers, appears to be related to the worship of the sun god as December 21, or Santo Tomás Day, is also the shortest day of the year.

Another blending of Christian and Mayan practices is seen in the Indian observances of All Saints' Day on November 1 and All Souls' Day on November 2. The village custom is for families to visit the graves of their dead bringing food, drink, and flowers, particularly marigolds, "the flowers of the dead." Candles are lit, and the visitors partake of *fiambre*, a special dish prepared for this occasion. Made with rice, meat, chicken, fish, and vegetables marinated in vinegar, *fiambre* is eaten cold like a salad. The entire day is spent at the cemetery in recall of loved ones.

At the cemetery in Santiago Sacatepéquez, a village northwest of the capital, an unusual custom that has developed is the flying

Overleaf, left: The Church of Santo Tomás in Chichicastenango
Right: A child with a can of incense
near the entrance of the cemetery at Chichicastenango

An informal Indian prayer altar showing candles and flower offerings

of huge, round kites made of bamboo and colored tissue paper and decorated with flags. The kites, which are designed with Mayan motifs, may be as large as twenty-five feet in diameter. Some believe that the flying of kites symbolizes the ascent of the soul heavenward. However, November is a time of strong, gusty winds in highland Guatemala in any case. As the winds herald the onset of the much-welcomed dry season, the kite flying on All Saints' Day may also signal that homage is being paid to the Mayan gods of nature.

In most Indian communities, great faith is placed in *brujos*, sorcerers or diviners. These practitioners are frequently called upon to place or remove curses, cast spells, concoct love potions, and foretell the future. Fused with these superstitions are many ancient Mayan practices. The gods are still sought out in caves, beside streams, and in wooded glens, where prayer ceremonies with incense, food offerings, and perhaps a chicken or other animal sacrifice may take place.

Geographical isolation, a limited land share, strong identity with one's community, and unique religious practices are not the only factors that separate the Indian from the rest of the population. Language has been another dividing line between the Indian and the Spanish-speaking Ladino. The four principal Mayan language groups of the highlands are Quiché, Mam, Cakchiquel, and Kekchí. In addition, there are a number of language subgroups and perhaps a hundred dialects.

Although education in Government-run schools is free and compulsory for children aged seven to fourteen, far fewer Indian than Ladino children attend. All instruction is in Spanish, and there are no bilingual classes to help Indian-speaking children bridge the language gap. Whether low attendance is due to Indian resistance to outside influences or to Government indifference toward educating the Indian is uncertain. Some Indians, like the merchant class of affluent storekeepers and other small entrepreneurs found in Quezaltenango, have welcomed a Spanish-language education for their children. The majority of poor Indians, however, may simply reject schooling because even young children are needed to help out in the family.

Estimates of the national illiteracy rate for Guatemala run from 50 to over 60 percent, while the Indian illiteracy rate in the country is believed to be at least 80 percent. Comparisons with the rest of Central America show similar national illiteracy rates, except for Costa Rica. Its egalitarian social features probably account for its low illiteracy rate of only 10 percent of the population.

Health care also divides the Indian from the Ladino. Although Government-run *puestos de salud*, or health centers, dot the highlands, the Indian rarely has access to the city-based clinics and hospitals, where more comprehensive health care is available. The local health center is usually staffed by a nurse or two and

receives a weekly or twice-weekly visit from a circuit doctor. Also, doctors-in-training generally serve for six months in the countryside during their graduating year at the university.

As in the case of public education, there is some built-in resistance to modern medical treatment. Villagers often prefer to consult a *curandero*, or lay healer, who will prescribe an herbal cure or perhaps use charms and incantations. If the visiting doctor relates well to the community, he may be able to introduce more effective remedies and, if he is open-minded, may even learn about some of the Indian herbal medicines that have curative value.

Throughout Central America, figures for infant mortality and malnutrition are high. But they may well be higher for the poor Ladino or mestizo population than for the Indian sector of Guatemala. National life expectancy is given as fifty-seven for Guatemala and Honduras, fifty-five for Nicaragua, sixty-three for El Salvador, and seventy for Costa Rica. Because no reliable statistics are available, it is impossible to say whether the life expectancy of the Guatemalan Indian is higher or lower than the national average.

In 1949, an attempt to improve nutrition for all of the isthmian countries was begun by INCAP, the Institute of Nutrition of Central America and Panama. Under the direction of Dr. Nevin S. Scrimshaw of the Massachusetts Institute of Technology, a program was set up to train local personnel and to teach the public about nutritional needs. A product called Incaparina was developed. This powdered corn-based substance, enriched with vitamins and proteins, can be added to cereal mixtures and other dishes or simply drunk mixed with water. Manufactured at

An Indian child who does not attend school
practicing the use of the tumpline for carrying heavy objects

101

a plant in Guatemala City, it is also widely distributed through-out Central America.

Despite the Indian's reluctance to merge with the rest of the Guatemalan population, changes are on the way. In the matter of dress, many Indians now wear mass-produced clothing like machine-made sweaters and high-heeled shoes for women and store-bought shirts and trousers for men and boys. Some clothing textiles, in traditional Indian patterns, are today woven on the foot loom, introduced by the Spanish, instead of on the backstrap loom. This newer loom, which can weave much wider fabrics, is worked with foot pedals. It is operated by men in small manufac-turing establishments, and its products are sold as yard goods in Indian markets.

Today there are few samples left of Indian textiles woven from naturally dyed cotton threads. The traditional dyes, used from classical Mayan times to the early twentieth century, included

The pedal-operated foot loom introduced by the Spanish

cochineal reds, indigo blues, and a purple extracted from shellfish. The colors glowed richly when new and mellowed softly when faded, making some of the modern synthetic colors seem garish in contrast.

Other mass-produced goods introduced in the last few decades are the plastic water jugs and other vessels that are bringing about a decline in Indian pottery making.

But the major influence that is fusing the Indian and Ladino worlds is the Indian's need for economic survival. Some families are drawn to the cities to look for work despite their unwillingness to exchange their natural environment for the noisy, mechanized urban scene. As poor newcomers, they live in hovels on the fringes of Guatemala City and other centers. Their links to the past are snapped and their family life is often broken up as young people, in particular, are tempted by the petty crime and other vices rampant in the urban shantytowns.

Most Indians who lack sufficient income have little recourse but to hire themselves out as seasonal farm workers on the coffee, sugar, cotton, and banana plantations that are owned by prosperous members of the Ladino population. In most cases, they must relocate in the lowlands, which means neglecting their small highland holdings, often for months at a time. Each year some 500,000 men, women, and children are signed up by Ladino contractors known as *contratistas,* or, less flatteringly, *enganchadores* (ensnarers). The workers, who are sometimes paid a modest advance to sign a low-wage agreement, are generally housed in open-sided sheds with no provisions for privacy, poor sanitary conditions, and minimal food. Some landowners are said to be making an effort to upgrade conditions.

Although the *repartimiento* no longer exists in Guatemala, many observers regard the Indian migrant farm worker as the victim of a modern forced-labor system brought on by economic need. It is estimated that 55 to 70 percent of the country's arable land is owned by 2 percent of the population. Yet attempts by short-lived reform governments to redistribute land have failed due to strong opposition from the large landowners.

While it is true that mechanized growing of sugarcane, bananas, and cotton could not be successfully carried out by small-scale farmers with no capital to invest, plantation wages have remained extremely low in the face of rising living costs. Many migrants receive as little as $1 a day. In 1980, after a painful strike, the pay of sugarcane cutters was raised for the first time in years to $3.20 per day.

Army service has been a major form of Ladinoization for the Indian. Young men are recruited for thirty months during which time they lose their identity with their heritage. Upon leaving the Army, many young Indians no longer feel comfortable in their villages and often experience a bitter sense of displacement and loss.

The Ladino, unlike the Indian, is not tied to a particular background and is much more mobile. Many Ladinos have found an Army career beneficial and have risen socially and economically through the ranks. While Ladinos may work at trades that Indians also pursue, like carpentry and bricklaying, they are not geographically or linguistically confined and can relate to other Ladinos anywhere in the country. Urban shopkeepers, salespeople, and service personnel, Government workers, teachers, and other professionals are Ladinos. Except for the Indian mayors of certain highland villages, Guatemala's political officials are Ladinos too.

The attitude of the Ladino toward the Indian varies. Better educated Ladinos have a deep appreciation of the Indian heritage and its cultural contributions. Guatemalans also acknowledge the economic benefit of the appeal that Indian dress, folk-

An Indian artisan's market in Guatemala City's Aurora Park,
designed to attract tourists

ways, religion, and handicrafts hold for tourists. Since 1967,
Guatemala's tourism has grown substantially, outpacing that of
its Central American neighbors. In 1979, a peak year, there were
500,000 foreign visitors, and tourism earned more foreign
exchange than any other business except coffee.

In general, however, the Ladino regards the Indian as lower in
status. Prosperous Ladinos who have Indian house servants often
address them in paternalistic and condescending terms, calling
an adult male "muchacho" (boy) or "chico" (little one). While
often employing the familiar *tu*, (meaning "you"), with Indians,
the Ladino frequently expects the Indian to use the respectful
usted alternative in response. However, in contacts with nonfam-
ily members of their own social class, upper-class Ladinos show
much formality and courtesy.

Sexual contacts between Ladino men and Indian women are
not uncommon. The offspring, even in cases where the father was

a *criollo*, will usually be brought up by the mother as if it were a pure-blooded Indian child. Among both Indians and lower-class Ladinos, there are many common-law marriages. But such arrangements between Indians are likely to be more stable. The Indian *matrimonio de hecho,* or common-law marriage, is generally formalized by verbal agreements, an exchange of gifts, and traditional marriage rites, even though there has been no visit to the registry office or the church.

The Ladino tends to be scornful of Indian superstitions and religious customs. Indian fiestas are a particular target of Ladino disapproval because of the large sums of money spent on firecrackers, music, costumes, and alcohol and because of the amount of drunkenness that usually ensues. Yet the manufacturers and vendors engaged in the nation's profitable fireworks industry are Ladinos, as are most of the traveling marimba orchestras that are hired to play at Indian festivities. Furthermore, Ladino sellers of food and drink and of plastic trinkets and toys do a thriving business at the numerous saint's days and Mayan religious festivals that fill the calendar year round.

The dances that are performed on these occasions are often enactments of past struggles between the Indians and their conquerors, with both groups wearing masks and costumes. The stiff, ritualized steps accompanied by drum beats are danced by men only. The wooden masks of the Indians are dark-complexioned and black-haired, while the Spaniards are represented as pink-fleshed and large-nosed with blond hair and moustaches. Interestingly, the conquerors are given their historical due, for the dances end with the Spaniards triumphing over the Indians.

Masks and costumes for a ritual dance
depicting Tecún Umán and Pedro de Alvarado;
on display at the Popol Vuh Museum in Guatemala City

The festivities of the Ladino population, which include a number of secular celebrations, are rather different in character. A town's observance of Guatemala's Independence Day on September 15, for example, might consist of a theatrical pageant performed by children, a parade, a basketball or soccer game, and Western-style dancing.

There are many predominantly Ladino religious celebrations. Antigua observes Holy Week with solemn processions of heavy platforms that carry images of the saints and Jesus. As in Spain, and especially in Seville, the weighty biers rest on the shoulders of scores of penitents. They are dressed in the robes and head coverings of the holy land at the time of the crucifixion.

The Easter ceremonies in Guatemala are renowned for the exquisite "street carpets" of colored sawdust in floral and religious designs that are laid in the path of the processions. Their intricate patterns are produced with stencils on the previous day. Throughout the night the sawdust is kept wetted down to prevent the particles from being blown away in the wind. Of course, the passage of the marching penitents the next day destroys the lovingly and painstakingly prepared carpet.

Christmas, the holiday that has most strongly captured the fancy of the Guatemalans, is observed by Ladinos with a blend of Spanish colonial and North American customs. The holiday season actually begins, however, on December 7 with a purely local custom known as Quema del Diablo, or Burning the Devil. Presumably the purpose of this event, which falls on the eve of the Day of Immaculate Conception, is to purify the household by ridding it of all the evils of the past year. Piles of trash and twigs, even old clothing, are dragged out into the streets and set afire at dusk. The leaping flames and dense smoke, which can reach choking proportions in Guatemala City, are accompanied by bursting firecrackers.

On December 16, the Christmas season begins in earnest with the *posada*, or reenactment of Mary and Joseph's search for a lodging place in which the Christ child will be born. The *posada,* which translates as "inn" or "lodging," is repeated for nine nights, until December 24. In Guatemala City, each evening soon after dark processions of children and teen-agers begin to march through the various neighborhoods. Bearing a small litter with the figures of the wandering Mary and Joseph, the children also carry pine torches or lanterns, beat rhythmically on turtle shells, and sing carols. As they proceed they knock on the doors of friends and neighbors begging admission for the weary pilgrims.

After an exchange of dialogue in song or poetry, the procession is invited to enter amid a burst of small firecrackers. The litter is placed on an altar decorated with flowers and leaves, and its bearers are offered fruit punch and cookies. A recent development that threatens to overtake the old customs is the *posada* by automobile, in which the beating of the turtle shell is replaced by the honking of the automobile horn.

The pre-Christmas firecracker market in Guatemala City

In the weeks before Nochebuena, or Christmas eve, Christmas markets spring up selling mangers made of straw, wreaths of pine cones, and bundles of silver-sprayed branches to be decorated with Christmas ornaments. Despite laws prohibiting the cutting of live trees, tall evergreens are available at street stalls for those willing and able to pay the price.

Along with the adoption of Santa Claus and the Christmas tree, Guatemalans remain loyal to the Spanish tradition of the *nacimiento*, or nativity scene. In homes, public buildings, and places of recreation, mangers are set up and filled with figures made of rag, clay, or wood that represent animals, shepherds, the Wise Men, Mary and Joseph, and the Christ child. The newborn Jesus, however, is not laid in its cradle until the midnight chimes that herald the arrival of Christmas.

The Nochebuena celebration includes massive explosions of firecrackers. A supper is served just after midnight. It consists of tamales filled with chicken, turkey, or pork, possibly sweetened with raisins and cinnamon, and accompanied by a warm fruit punch. Gifts are exchanged on this occasion or on Christmas Day. The *piñata*, a clay jug covered with ruffled paper and filled with candies and other goodies, is not as indispensable to *posada* and Nochebuena parties in Guatemala as it is in Mexico. It is, however, popular at birthday parties where the blindfolded guests poke at the dangling *piñata* with a stick in order to break it and release its contents.

Christmas Day is marked with more barrages of fireworks. They are climaxed only by the massive bursts of rockets that greet the New Year on December 31.

Sports are another popular diversion. A favorite of the Ladinos is baseball, which was introduced way back in 1880 by the United States companies that developed banana growing in Central America. The United Fruit Company, in particular, actively promoted baseball from 1900 on. At the same time, the Spanish spectacle of bullfighting began to decline in popularity. The bullfight has never been as popular in Central America as in Mexico.

Movies and television are the most widespread forms of entertainment in the larger population centers. Guatemala City has dozens of movie theaters and five television channels. Both Spanish-language and American films are shown, the latter with Spanish subtitles. TV fare includes situation comedies, action series, and old movies from the United States, all titled in Spanish, along with domestic *telenovelas*, or soap operas, and specialty and news features.

Cultural events—concerts, recitals, ballet and folkloric dance, drama, and art films, performed by both Guatemalan and visiting artists—are presented in the capital. Many of these programs are given at the new National Theater complex built atop the hill of the old San José Fortress.

An intriguing aspect of life in the capital is the great variety of foods available. They range from tacos and enchiladas (tortillas wrapped around spicy chicken, meat, or cheese fillings) to *ham-*

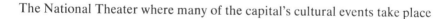

The National Theater where many of the capital's cultural events take place

burguesas, American style. Guatemala City has branches of such fast-food chains as McDonald's, Wimpy's, and Hardees, as well as Pizza Hut. In addition, there are locally owned fried-chicken chains known as Pollo Campero and Mister Pollo. Ham-and-cheese sandwiches, called *mixtos*, are available at almost all informal eating spots around the country.

Surprisingly, Chinese restaurants are numerous, even outside the capital. Guatemala City diners can also find seafood and steak houses, Swiss, German, Italian, French, Spanish, and Argentine restaurants. At the same time, hotels and restaurants offer *típico* meals. A Guatemalan-style breakfast would include eggs with a spicy ranchero sauce, mashed black beans with tangy, crumbly white cheese, fried *plátano* (plaintain, or cooking banana), tortillas, and coffee. A *plato típico* at lunch or dinner features *carne asada*, a strip of grilled beefsteak served with two sauces, one of tomatoes and onions and the other fiery with chili peppers. Rice, black beans, white cheese, fried *plátano*, guacamole (avocado mashed with onions and chili) and tortillas make up the rest of the *plato*.

Other dishes typical of Guatemalan cuisine are black bean soup, *chiles rellenos* (large mild peppers stuffed with meat), and *chuchitos*, which are similar to tamales. A popular vegetable is the güisquil (or huisquil), a delicate-flavored squash that varies in size from that of a lemon to a very large pear and in color from pale to dark green. A favorite among all Guatemalans, both Indian and Ladino, it is usually served steamed.

Because of its rather strongly defined Indian and Ladino sectors, Guatemala has been called a pluralistic or dualistic society. There are also two very small ethnic subgroups that live on the geographical fringes of Guatemala, even more insulated from the mainstream than the *indígenas* of the highland fastnesses.

The first are the Lacandones, who inhabit the northern and

western Petén bordering on Mexico. The Lacandón people are Mayans who avoided subjugation under the Spanish by reverting to a semiwild way of life. They have continued to resist authority and live today by hunting, fishing, and raising small patches of maize near their scattered jungle campsites. Their dwellings, clothing, and implements are crude, and their appearance is characterized by their long, matted hair.

Almost diagonally across the Petén, on the Caribbean coast of the department of Izabal, lives the second group, Guatemala's blacks, or Caribs. A large portion of this population is concentrated in the town of Lívingston. Descended from Caribbean Indians and African slaves, the Caribs speak Spanish plus a West Indian patois. Some also speak English due to the proximity of Belize. Their foods tend to be Caribbean, consisting largely of tubers, fish, and tropical fruits. A local specialty is the home-made candy of fresh coconut and brown sugar that is hawked by women vendors in wide-brimmed straw hats at the town dock.

Lívingston was named for the Louisiana jurist whose judicial code was adopted by Mariano Gálvez in the 1830's. As the town is inaccessible by road, it must be reached by boat either from Puerto Barrios or via the Río Dulce, which flows twenty miles from the outlet of Lake Izabal to the Caribbean. Lívingston was once an active port to which the coffee growers of Alta Verapaz shipped their coffee by way of the Río Polochic. Many of the coffee *fincas*, or estates, were operated by Germans in the years between 1869 and the Second World War. But coffee cultivation gradually shifted to the Pacific slope region. Also, in the early 1940's, the Guatemalan Government expropriated the holdings of many of the German farmers, who were believed to have Nazi sympathies.

Today Lívingston is a tranquil tropical town of about 3000, its main street lined with waving palms and houses painted in

The beachfront in the town of Lívingston

pinks, blues, and greens. The hill on which the governor's mansion once stood leads down to a long, curving beachfront dotted with thatch-roofed houses, each with its *cayuco*, or dugout canoe, for fishing in the gentle waters of the Bay of Amatique, the inlet of the Caribbean.

Also on the Caribbean coast are two of Guatemala's main commercial ports, Puerto Barrios and the newer and more efficient Puerto Matías de Gálvez, still usually referred to by its old name of Santo Tomás de Castilla. The main shipping center

114

on the Pacific coast is Puerto San José. However, deepwater harbors are rare along the Pacific shoreline, and large vessels cannot enter this port. Their freight must be transferred to smaller boats to be landed.

Guatemala's national economy, once dependent on cacao, indigo, and cochineal, began to boom during the latter half of the nineteenth century with the introduction of coffee growing. Brought to Costa Rica in the 1830's (from Cuba and Haiti where it was first cultivated in the New World), the crop soon expanded to all five Central American countries.

In Guatemala, the combination of excellent climate and easily pulverized volcanic soil made ideal coffee-growing conditions in such widely scattered places as Alta Verapaz, Antigua, and the volcanic slopes of Lake Atitlán. Indian-held lands, for which there were no formal documents of title, were in many cases taken over by the ambitious Ladino planters. Today coffee is Guatemala's number-one commercial earner of foreign income and represents 45 percent of the country's total agricultural export. Coffee growing and processing employs two million workers, over a quarter of the population. Yet this degree of concentration on a single crop can be hazardous, as when world coffee prices fell from a previous high in the early 1980's.

Cotton, sugar, cattle products, and bananas, in that order, are next after coffee in agricultural earning power. Cotton was an indigenous crop of minor export value until the United States' Civil War of 1861 to 1865, when foreign demand rose because of the devastation of the American cotton-growing South. Later, following the Second World War, the market for Guatemalan cotton boomed and output has since increased steadily. In recent decades, Guatemala's cotton growers have been criticized by environmentalists for their heavy use of DDT and its effect on cotton-field workers.

While Guatemala can most properly be called a "coffee republic," a number of other Central American countries have been dubbed "banana republics" because of their economic dependence on that crop. Also, their national politics were dominated by the foreign-based banana growers. The most prominent of them was the United Fruit Company, which was established in 1899 upon the merger of two smaller American companies and became active in Guatemala and elsewhere on the isthmus.

Whether operating their own plantations on large tracts of coastal land that governments had given them to develop, or whether buying from local growers at company-controlled prices, there is no question that UFCO wielded monopolistic powers. Furthermore, the company did not hesitate to step into local political affairs and labor matters to ensure the continued profitability of its enterprise.

At the same time, UFCO improved certain features of its Central American client states, building highways, railroads, and ports. It even made such cultural contributions in Guatemala as the development of the archeological site of Quiriguá and the reconstruction of the postclassic ruins of Zaculeu near the city of Huehuetenango.

However, in 1964, for reasons of declining profitability and fears of political instability, UFCO closed out its operations in Guatemala and subsequently reduced its holdings in Central America. Today the company is known as United Brands and has banana-growing operations only in Honduras, Costa Rica, and Panama. Guatemala's banana plantations, located mainly in the Caribbean lowlands, are independently operated.

Efforts are continually being made in Guatemala to develop new export crops. Two recent entrants have been macadamia nuts and cardamom seeds. Yet, as more land is taken over for growing cash crops for foreign markets, less is left for domestic food growing. One unfortunate result has been that Guatemala recently has begun importing corn and other food staples.

Mineral and oil wealth also contribute to the national economy. Nickel has been an important export over the years, while newfound oil deposits in the Petén indicate that Guatemala may share the extensive oil-reserve basin already being exploited on the Mexican side of the border. Proven Guatemalan reserves are said to be 33 to 35 million barrels, while estimated reserves may run to 5 or 6 billion barrels, enough to rank Guatemala as a top oil-producing nation. A pipeline already runs from the southern Petén fields to Puerto Barrios.

As the extraction of untapped oil is a costly procedure, the Government has invited foreign companies to make bids for exploration. However, it exacts a profitable return for its vital resource and asks that the companies promise to build roads, hospitals, and schools at the exploration sites. At the same time, the Government is trying to develop a strategy for restricting its oil output so that it can be used as a bargaining tool in an increasingly oil-hungry world. Already, by 1980, Guatemala's oil was earning almost as much foreign revenue as its coffee.

Although industrial development has lagged in Guatemala, recent years have seen an influx of pharmaceutical plants owned by multinational corporations. The companies were attracted to Guatemala by low-cost labor and tax concessions. Other industries that presently serve domestic and/or export markets are the manufacturing of textiles, clothing, and furniture; leather processing; food freezing and canning; meat packing; sugar refining; flour milling; beer brewing; and the manufacture of batteries and glass containers.

Compared to its Central American neighbors, Guatemala has enjoyed a booming economy since the early 1960's, and its national income is the highest of the five nations. Still, its per

117

Public washtubs for those who do not have running water

capita income is estimated at only $900 a year as opposed to $1600 a year in Costa Rica. Where does the national wealth, derived largely from the labor of poor peasants, go?

The answer is that its wealthy recipients channel it into profitable domestic and foreign investment. It does not filter down to the working class. Within Guatemala, profits are directed into ventures like banking, real estate, tourism, and light industry. As a result, some new jobs have opened up, yet workers' wages remain low.

In fact, as the Guatemalan economy has prospered, its poor people have grown even poorer. Inflation is currently running high, but wages have risen so slowly that purchasing power keeps falling. The enormous prosperity of Guatemala's upper class as opposed to the rising expectations of its middle and lower classes has engendered much bitterness. At the same time, the Government has not stepped up its social programs. Social security exists for only a portion of the workers and in a very limited form, and there is no comprehensive public welfare system. The Government admits that "the task of national uplift is formidable and the country has a long way to go in improving the life standard of its citizens."

But the patience of those who have championed the cause of the poor and the socially repressed is wearing thin. By the early 1980's, two Central American nations—Nicaragua and El Salvador—had entered periods of political turmoil and sharp social upheaval. How long could Guatemala, already torn by a submerged but violent struggle between the right and the left, resist the rumblings rocking its foundations?

IV

Guatemala and Its Neighbors

Guatemala today claims worldwide attention for two principal reasons. One is its richly preserved Indian culture, which provides us with a unique pageant of living history. The other is its troubled political situation set against the background of its Central American neighbors.

These two aspects of the Guatemalan scene are related. Wealthy landowning and business interests supported by a right-wing government are dedicated to the preservation of a traditional social and economic system. As in the past, this system is designed to keep the large laboring population of Indians and other poor workers relatively voiceless politically and dependent economically.

Present-day Guatemala seems caught in the web of the past. As in the preconquest Mayan era, as in the Spanish colonial period, political power is concentrated in the hands of a small elite group. So powerful is the ruling leadership that voices of moderation have not been recognized and have no official status in the Government or secure legal position in the country. All too often, advocates of liberalization have been accused of being Communists or Communist sympathizers and have even become the victims of political murders. In this extremist atmosphere,

Guatemala has not been truly free to work out its destiny, to achieve the benefits of an open and just society.

Historically, the achievement of independence from Spanish rule did not lead to political ideas of democracy. Perhaps the only real change resulting from Guatemala's liberation from Spain in 1821 was that leaders of ordinary rather than aristocratic background gained the opportunity to come to power.

One such leader was José Rafael Carrera, an illiterate Ladino and a guerrilla fighter from the mountains, who became president of Guatemala in 1844. Although Carrera's origins were among the poor and the common people, he espoused the Conservative prochurch line of the old Spanish upper class. He restored the mandatory payment of taxes to the church, reinstituted religious education, and championed the right of the large landowners to exploit both Indian lands and labor. Except for one three-year interruption, Carrera's authoritarian rule continued until his death in 1865. Then Vicente Cerna, his personally chosen successor, carried on Carrera's domestic policies and also his active support of Conservative leaders elsewhere in Central America until 1871.

During Carrera's regime the United States began to insert itself into Central America. Although Guatemala was only indirectly involved at the time, it too was influenced by American activities in the years that immediately followed the California gold strike of 1848. Eager to reach the west coast, many fortyniners from the eastern seaboard took advantage of a route across the Central American isthmus, either through the watery lowlands of southern Nicaragua or across the jungles of Panama. Cornelius Vanderbilt, the American railroad and shipping magnate, offered a Nicaraguan passage by means of his newly organized Accessory Transit Company. His passengers sailed to the

Caribbean coast of Nicaragua, crossed the isthmus by riverboat and lake steamer, and finally proceeded by oceangoing vessel to California.

In 1855, other powerful American entrepreneurs completed a railroad across Panama. Already thoughts of a canal were in the minds of many. But, as Panama belonged to Colombia, most schemes revolved around the idea of linking the natural waterways of independent Nicaragua.

Various groups challenged Vanderbilt's bid for influence in Nicaragua, and, in 1855, one such group raised money to finance a Nicaraguan campaign under the leadership of a political adventurer by the name of William Walker. Walker, a Tennessee-born ex-journalist and onetime medical student, was given

San Juan del Sur in the watery lowlands of southern Nicaragua

arms and ammunition to overthrow the Conservative Government of Nicaragua and help install a Liberal regime that would be more receptive to a foreign investment and development program.

Walker's well-financed military campaign succeeded, but instead of turning over the government to the Liberals, as planned, he stepped into the presidency of Nicaragua himself in 1856. Carrera, the Guatemalan strongman, sent troops to Nicaragua and helped end Walker's brief term in office in 1857. Although Walker returned to the United States, he foolishly went back to Central America shortly thereafter. In 1860, he was executed by a firing squad in Honduras.

Also during José Rafael Carrera's rule in Guatemala difficulties arose with Great Britain. In 1859, Carrera agreed that if the British Government would build a railroad from Guatemala City to a Guatemalan seaport on the Caribbean, Guatemala would cede its claims to Belize to Britain. A treaty was signed, and in 1862 Belize became a British crown colony and was given the official name of British Honduras. The promised railroad, however, was never built. Guatemala thus renewed its claims to Belize and maintains them to this day.

In general, the several decades of Conservative rule ushered in by Carrera left the Guatemalan economy in a state of decline. A strong contributing factor was the loss of the indigo and cochineal trade when aniline dyes came on the market after 1850.

Opposition to Cerna grew, and in 1871 he was unseated with some help from Benito Juárez, the leader of the reform movement in Mexico. A Liberal Government was installed, and the presidency went to Justo Rufino Barrios, who has been accorded a place in history as El Reformador of Guatemala. A skeletal metal tower, reminiscent of the Eiffel Tower in Paris and known as the Torre del Reformador (Tower of the Reformer), soars

above one of the capital's main thoroughfares. The bell on top of the tower is rung on June 30, the anniversary of the 1871 Liberal takeover.

Following in the tradition of Mariano Gálvez, the Liberal leader of the 1830's, the new Liberal Government reduced the authority of the church and instituted freedom of worship and a public education program. But it did not bring about any real social reforms. Its emphasis was on material progress and economic growth, and there its achievements were considerable. Roads, ports, and communications were developed, and a railroad was begun. A banking system was established, and capital was made available to large-scale coffee growers and other entrepreneurs, including some members of the middle class.

At the same time, Guatemala remained a republic without democracy. Nothing was done to check the takeover of Indian lands for coffee *fincas* or to liberalize the treatment of the Indians and other laborers. Barrios ruled as a dictator. Brandishing a horsewhip, he once asserted, "*This* is the constitution I govern by."

Like the Conservative Carrera, the Liberal Barrios attempted to bring the leaders of the other Central American states under his influence and envisioned a Central American political union under his direct control. He was killed in 1885 in El Salvador trying to realize that goal.

In the decades that followed, the Liberal Governments' policies of economic development continued and were most often achieved with the help of United States companies. Frequently, however, the means used involved economic domination and

The Torre del Reformador,
which commemorates the Liberal takeover of 1871

125

political repression. By 1900, major American businesses led by the banana companies had established themselves in Central America. To protect their investments, they did not hesitate to call on the military forces of the United States to put down insurrections, keep friendly rulers in power, and guard the lives and property of American citizens in Central America.

In 1903, the United States Government itself became militarily involved in the region when it plotted the uprising by means of which Panama gained its independence from Colombia. This maneuver, carried out with the full knowledge of President Theodore Roosevelt, was undertaken for the specific purpose of building a canal across Panama. Victory in the Spanish-American War of 1898 had given the United States new possessions in the Caribbean—Puerto Rico and a Cuban naval base—as well as the Philippines in the Pacific. It now wanted to link these possessions with a convenient water route.

Newly independent Panama yielded up to the United States a ten-mile-wide Canal Zone that was, in effect, an American Government outpost on its soil. The actual building of the canal, which was completed in 1914, brought certain benefits to the region. Numerous Panamanian and other workers were given employment, and yellow fever and malaria were eradicated. But, in the long run, the isthmian countries derived comparatively little economic advantage from the waterway. Its benefits went mainly to those developed countries of the world that used its facilities to expand and enrich their international trade.

As the twentieth century advanced, the growing United States presence in Central America began to have a strong polarizing effect. Local citizens became divided into sharply antagonistic

The Panama Canal, completed in 1914

political camps. On the one hand, there were those who regarded American intervention as neocolonialism, a form of imperialist domination. Among this group, there developed a rampant Yankeephobia. On the other hand, those in positions of wealth and power enjoyed the economic and political advantages of the American connection. As a result, the governments of Guatemala and other Central American republics became increasingly repressive as they sought to silence would-be agitators and revolutionaries.

In 1931, the autocratic General Jorge Ubico Castañeda took office in Guatemala. Many Guatemalans welcomed Ubico, and some still venerate him as a harsh but just president. Most of his predecessors of the past thirty years had been corrupt and ineffectual. In contrast, Ubico is credited with having restored stability and national pride to Guatemala. During his regime, the huge, impressive National Palace was built to house the headquarters of government. Constructed in a combination of Spanish colonial and Moorish styles and covered with pale green stone, the Palace faces on the Parque Central of Guatemala City. Residents of *la capital* or Guate, as the city is known, sometimes refer to the National Palace as the *guacamolón*, or "big guacamole," because of its light green color.

As a Liberal in economic matters, Ubico extended tax and tariff exemptions to the United Fruit Company and improved roads and public works. He also built a modern military machine and during the Second World War showed his loyalty to the United States by confiscating many of the German coffee *fincas*. Ubico was a strong disciplinarian, who did not flinch at inflicting cruel punishments and even torture to hold crime and left-wing activity in check. It was said that during his regime thieves were punished by having their fingers chopped off. The press was censored, and he suspended the clause in the constitution forbidding re-election. Thus entrenched, he remained in office until 1944 when he was forced to resign.

As the Second World War drew to a close, a strong wave of opposition to tyranny began sweeping the globe. Demands were heard for social reforms, for the recognition of human rights and freedoms, and for an end to colonialism. In Guatemala in 1945, this new wave brought to power Juan José Arévalo Bermejo, an educator and philosopher, who had lived in exile during the Ubico regime. Warmly backed by students and workers, Arévalo began to implement his program known as "spiritual socialism," which emphasized labor and social reforms, the spread of literacy, and the expansion of voting rights.

Arévalo was also a nationalist, who opposed United States influence and economic domination in Guatemala. Although he was not a Communist, his administration did attract leftists, particularly in the area of labor organization. Few non-Communists

The National Palace in Guatemala City, built during the Ubico regime

in Latin America, where labor had seldom been permitted to organize, had any experience of this procedure. In 1949, the long-suppressed Communist Party of Guatemala (PCG) was legally recognized. The landowners and UFCO were alarmed, particularly when organized labor struck for wage increases.

Nonetheless, Guatemalans favored minimum-wage laws, medical care for workers, and better housing and schooling, and so in 1951 they elected Jácobo Arbenz Guzmán president. Arbenz, whose non-Hispanic name derived from his Swiss father, moved Guatemala into an even more anti-American stance when he criticized American intervention in Korea. At home, he undertook a land-reform program, proposing to put unused UFCO lands in western Guatemala into the hands of small farmers so they could grow domestic food crops.

The Arbenz government offered to pay $600,000 for the lands, a price higher than their assessed value. But UFCO demanded reparations of over $15,000,000 for their unimproved properties. Arbenz, therefore, expropriated some of the UFCO holdings for land redistribution, and he further antagonized the banana company by supporting a strike of Honduran banana workers against it. The lands of compensated Guatemalan landowners, too, went into the redistribution, which benefited 100,000 peasants.

By 1954, Arbenz faced a standoff not only with UFCO but with the United States Government. Under President Dwight Eisenhower and Secretary of State John Foster Dulles, the United States was fighting the "cold war" with its former ally, the Soviet Union. Ever on the alert for Communist infiltration, the United States saw Guatemala not as a reformist nation attempting to redress social ills, but as a country going Communist.

Although Arbenz was not a Communist, his wife was a member of the party. Also, after the United States refused to sell

An Indian woman being interviewed for social assistance
under one of the public welfare programs
introduced under the Arévalo and Arbenz presidencies

Guatemala arms, it began to buy them from Communist eastern
Europe. In these circumstances, the investments of UFCO and
other United States businesses appeared to be threatened. And
so, their mission seen as one of nipping Communism in the bud,
the CIA and the United States Marine Corps lent their assistance
to Colonel Carlos Castillo Armas, who had been waiting in exile
in Honduras.

Leading a revolutionary force of right-wing Guatemalans,

Castillo Armas toppled the Arbenz presidency on June 27, 1954. Arbenz escaped and fled to Mexico, where he died in 1971, and Castillo Armas assumed the presidency.

Between 1954 and 1957, when Castillo Armas was assassinated, the country returned to the repressionist policies of Ubico and his predecessors. Civil rights were suspended for security purposes, labor union activity was stifled, and the UFCO and private holdings were returned to their former owners. The peasants were evicted with weak promises of settlement elsewhere. Vice-President Richard Nixon, of the United States, who visited Guatemala in 1954 after Castillo Armas took office, saw no reason to lament the changes and, in fact, endorsed the regime of Castillo Armas as a bulwark against Communism.

Since Guatemala's brief experience with the Arévalo and Arbenz administrations, sharp political divisions have endured in the nation. Although suspected Arbenz sympathizers were jailed by Castillo Armas, Yankeephobia and leftist guerrilla activity were not stamped out. Nor did Guatemalans begin to give any real consideration to the possibility of a moderate type of government, neither Communist nor conservative, in which the rights of both landowners *and* peasants, capitalists *and* workers, would be recognized.

The United States, which recognizes the rights of labor, might have encouraged such development in Guatemala. But instead the old colonialist attitude prevailed. The United States used its influence to extract raw materials and to protect and expand American investments and markets, even at the cost of supporting corrupt, dictatorial leaders. The fallacy of this policy was stunningly brought to light in 1959 when Fulgencio Batista, the pro-United States Cuban dictator, who had long supported Yankee imperialism in his island nation, was toppled by the revolutionary army of Fidel Castro. Now the United States had a

Communist country, with direct ties to the Soviet Union, in its Caribbean "front yard."

The 1960's, with their heightened fears of Cuban-directed left-wing activity and their rumors of the return of Arévalo to Guatemala, saw the rise of such right-wing terrorist organizations as The White Hand and An Eye for an Eye. So sharply to the right did the pendulum swing that the president was replaced in 1963 by a military dictator.

Violence in the form of guerrilla activity and urban terrorism

Fidel Castro addressing the United Nations General Assembly in 1979

erupted frequently in Guatemala during the latter part of the 1960's. Even foreign officials who appeared not to have been directly involved were endangered. United States Ambassador John Gordon Mein and two American military attachés were killed in 1968 as was the West German ambassador in 1970. Among labor organizers, student activists, teachers, peasant leaders, and Catholic clergymen and social workers, there were numerous disappearances. It was presumed they had become the victims of right-wing "death squads" or of the Army itself. And as the murders of those labeled Communist—or Communist sympathizers—escalated, so did the murders of right-wing political figures, presumably at the hands of the leftists.

This activity continued into the 1970's. Yet, on the surface, Guatemala appeared a relatively tranquil and stable society, particularly for those not engaged in politics or social reform. Tourism was healthy, and the presidential line of succession was orderly.

According to Guatemala's 1965 constitution, the president and vice-president are elected for a four-year term, and the president is not permitted to succeed himself by immediate re-election. A cabinet is appointed by the president, and a single-chamber legislature is elected by the people. Citizens of both sexes, aged eighteen and over, have the vote regardless of race or religion, and there is no literacy requirement. Voting is, in fact, mandatory, with penalties imposed for not voting. In practice, however, less than half the Guatemalan population usually votes, and voting cards are seldom checked for lapses. The 1965 constitution divides the Government into separate executive, legislative, and judicial branches, and the president serves as commander in chief of the armed forces. The Communist Party is outlawed.

Guatemala, however, is not a single-party state. As of 1981, there were eight registered parties that covered a political spectrum from the extreme right to nominally left-of-center. In actuality, there are usually only three or four presidential candidates, as coalitions are formed among the parties, and the winner is most often the candidate endorsed by the powerful right-of-center parties. This factor, plus the general unresponsiveness of the legislators to the public, may account for the high degree of voter apathy in Guatemala.

The first president of the 1970's was Colonel Carlos Arana Osorio, who served from 1970 to 1974. Arana was a conservative from Oriente, who had been active in the pursuit of leftists in his own region. As president he continued a strong anti-Communist campaign nationwide.

The 1974 election of General Kjell Laugerud García (whose name stems from his part-Norwegian parentage) was contested by the presidential candidate of a left-of-center coalition, who claimed to have been the winner. However, despite accusations of fraud in the ballot counting, Laugerud was declared president. During his term some progressive trends emerged; new labor unions and rural cooperatives were formed. Unfortunately, the disastrous earthquake of 1976 claimed priorities that prevented the implementation of public programs that had been planned.

The 1978 election brought General Romeo Lucas García to office. His vice-president was Francisco Villagrán Kramer, a civilian and a reformist who had been connected with the Laugerud administration. But, under President Lucas, Guatemala took a sharp swing to the right. It was sparked by a combination of factors: the alarm felt by Guatemalan business leaders and landowners at the growing number of popular movements in the country, and revolutionary events in Nicaragua that generated a heightened fear of encroaching Communism.

As a result, new secret organizations to fight Communism

were formed. Although not openly sanctioned by the Government, they almost certainly had its approval and quite possibly its support. A renewed rash of political murders began to take place. As in the years between 1966 and 1974, the victims included trade union organizers, activist students and professors from the capital's San Carlos University, and other social reformers.

Among those individuals targeted was a respected political figure, Manuel Colom Argueta, a former mayor of Guatemala City. Colom Argueta had just succeeded in getting his left-of-center political party, the United Revolutionary Front (FUR), officially registered when he was assassinated in March 1979. He was believed to have been murdered by the far right, but his killers were never apprehended by the police.

Other targets, in this case openly hunted by the Army, included the several well-organized guerrilla groups operating in the countryside and presumably working with the Indians to obtain their social and economic betterment. Increasingly, these groups were attacking and murdering landowners and farm superintendents. Often Indian farm workers and other peasants were caught in the middle, becoming the innocent victims of the Army's campaigns against the guerrillas.

Business leaders and other conservatives were also being murdered. In May 1980, Alberto Habie Mishaan, the owner of a large textile plant in Guatemala City and president of an anti-Communist propaganda organization, was assassinated. Responsibility was openly claimed by the Guatemalan Workers' Party (PGT), an unregistered political party that is considered a thin smokescreen for the banned Communist Party.

A church in Guatemala City severely damaged by the 1976 earthquake

Amid this atmosphere of political violence, the Lucas presidency did make some efforts to introduce social improvements. A program of road construction, public works, extended electrification, and increased educational and health facilities was announced. The Government also began carrying out a resettlement project aimed at moving 20,000 poor Ladino peasants from Oriente to the state-owned Northern Transverse Strip, which runs along the northerly limits of the departments of Alta Verapaz, Quiché, and Huehuetenango. Since these lands, although not necessarily legally titled, were traditionally considered to be Indian territory, there was some concern that Indian community leaders might object to this land reform program. To maintain good public relations with the Indians, the Government frequently pointed out that Lucas García, who came from Cobán in Alta Verapaz, was himself of Indian background and that he spoke perfect Kekchí.

To aid the unemployed and the underemployed, the Government also encouraged the growth of the industrial sector by offering tax advantages in certain free zones. These zones were located away from crowded urban centers like Guatemala City, which has a fast-growing population of a million and a half. The decentralization of industry was intended to increase employment around the country and to help equalize incomes.

Although Guatemala is often thought of as a country that is characterized by extremes of wealth and poverty, there is evidence of a substantial and growing middle class. Mainly urban, this group is composed of small-business owners, professional people, and Government personnel. Although income statistics are not available, Government representatives point to the

Government offices in the capital's Centro Civico
that give employment to the growing middle class

increasing consumption of manufactured goods to prove the extent of middle-class purchasing power. One example offered is the import of medium-priced automobiles. Five thousand Toyotas alone were sold in Guatemala in 1979, assumedly to middle-class consumers.

Another positive factor during the Lucas presidency was said to be the freedom that the press enjoyed. It was true that the capital's principal newspapers—*Prensa Libre, El Gráfico,* and *El Imparcial*—reported the politically motivated kidnappings and assassinations that took place almost daily. However, their editorial pages generally dealt with safe subjects like the lamentable increase in the number of traffic deaths and the need for cleaner city streets. Behind the scenes, violence had been directed at journalists of both leftist and rightist persuasions. In August 1980, the conservative editor of *El Imparcial* was murdered in what appeared to be a retaliatory action by the left.

In the final months of 1980, Vice-President Villagrán Kramer, seeing little hope of implementing his reformist ideas in the Lucas Government, resigned his office and left the country.

There are a number of reasons, both long-term and immediate, for the repression and violence that appear to threaten the stability of Guatemala, possibly in the near future. Historically, there is the Spanish colonial pattern of a rigid class structure maintained through oligarchic control, absolute power concentrated in the hands of a ruling few. Another historic influence is that of the United States. The paternalistic policies of the Colossus of the North have often brought about more problems in Central America than existed prior to American intervention.

A more immediate threat comes from Communist Cuba,

Middle-class consumers thronging the busy shopping streets of Guatemala City

which is believed to have had an effect, direct or indirect, on the destabilization of both Nicaragua and El Salvador in 1979. Whether the revolutionary activity in those countries was carried out by home-grown or Cuban-directed rebels is very difficult to say. Certainly nationally based Communism existed in Guatemala prior to the 1959 Communist takeover of Cuba, as during the Arbenz presidency of 1951 to 1954.

In any case, Guatemala's vulnerability lies in its own nonegalitarian society in which Indians, peasants, and workers at the bottom of the economic heap provide a ready issue for leftist agitators and revolutionaries to exploit. As the five nations of Central America, with a total population of twenty million people, occupy an area that is only the size of the state of California, Guatemala's fears are well justified. Certainly the upsurge of right-wing repression in Guatemala from 1979 on is linked to the fear of becoming "another Nicaragua."

The events in Nicaragua began in 1978 when a group of revolutionaries who called themselves Sandinistas (after Augusto César Sandino, a guerrilla leader assassinated in 1934) rose up successfully against President Anastasio Somoza Debayle. In power since 1967, he was the third member of the Somoza dynasty to rule the country, ruthlessly exploiting its resources to amass a huge family fortune. In July 1979, Somoza was forced to flee and went into exile in Paraguay, where he was assassinated in September 1980.

The new Nicaraguan Government was headed by a junta, or ruling committee, that promised a political system in which all groups would be represented. The junta nationalized key businesses and converted large plantations into state-run communes (rather than turning them over to poor peasant owners who could not have maintained production). At the same time, the Nicaraguan private sector continued to control about 60 percent of the economy, and dissenting political parties were permitted.

Although the United States had supported the Somozas for over forty years, the administration of President Jimmy Carter gave the Nicaraguan junta economic aid in the hope that it could be held to a moderate rather than a pro-Communist course. However, the administration of President Ronald Reagan, which took power in 1981, was less inclined to offer friendship to the junta because of its ties with Cuba.

With the fall of Somoza, relations between Guatemala and Nicaragua deteriorated rapidly. Guatemalan right-wingers viewed Nicaragua as no better than a "Cuban puppet" and a dangerous exporter of revolution in Central America.

Another upheaval of deep concern to Guatemala has been the

Nicaragua's President Anastasio Somoza Debayle
at a United Nations luncheon in 1971

civil war in El Salvador following the overthrow of the country's president, General Carlos Humberto Romero, in October 1979. As the smallest and most overcrowded isthmian country, with a population density of over 400 persons per square mile, El Salvador had over 200,000 landless peasants and suffered extreme poverty. Many Salvadorans had migrated illegally into less populous Honduras until 1969, when that country closed its border. Ruled by the military since 1932, El Salvador was economically dominated by Los Catorce, the so-called Fourteen Families, although their number actually exceeded fourteen.

Following the presidential coup, a junta composed of progressive young military officers and civilian leaders took over the Salvadoran Government. But their attempts to gain the trust of the leftist opposition failed, and by early 1980 the junta had changed its personnel and moved to the right. Its policies, especially on the important issue of land reform, did not satisfy the leftist guerrillas or the far right, and both factions threatened to overthrow it. At the same time, repression and political violence at the hands of "death squads" and Government security forces became as severe as under the regime of General Romero.

Especially shocking were the murders of four American women—three nuns and a Catholic lay worker—in December 1980. The women's bodies were later revealed to have been secretly buried with the complicity of members of the Salvadoran security forces. A campaign of terror had long been conducted by the extreme right against priests and nuns who worked among the poor and advocated social reform. In March 1980, Roman Catholic Archbishop Oscar Arnulfo Romero, had been murdered. Land-reform workers, both Salvadoran and American, had also met violent death from the right in El Salvador.

Poverty in poor, densely populated El Salvador

In 1981, under the Reagan administration, the United States stepped up its military aid to the junta, defending its stance on the ground that El Salvador was being threatened with Communism exported directly from Cuba and the Soviet Union. Many Americans, however, were concerned that military support of the right-of-center junta would only encourage the extreme right and provoke the left, causing a deepening crisis and perhaps a Central American regional war involving the United States. The Salvador: n junta itself asked for more economic rather than military aid as a means of maintaining popular support and resisting its internal enemies. Informed observers from other countries around the world saw the conflict in El Salvador as rooted not in Communist agitation but in social injustice.

The conservative Guatemalan Government has been sympathetic to the right-wing elements in El Salvador. Many wealthy Salvadorans have fled to neighboring Guatemala, using it as a base from which to counter leftist influence and activity in their country.

Relations between Guatemala and the remaining two countries of the Central American community—Honduras and Costa Rica—have long been friendly to neutral. However, these relations threaten to be jeopardized by the crises in Nicaragua and El Salvador.

Honduras, unlike El Salvador, is a fairly large isthmian country with a relatively small population. While its national income is among the lowest in Central America, it has not suffered social and economic pressures as intense as those of its land-squeezed neighbor. Although much Honduran land is in the hands of foreign banana companies, a fairly successful agrarian reform pro-

In Honduras, where extensive banana production
is in the hands of foreign companies

146

gram has been carried out by the Government since 1975. Also rural cooperatives and trade unions have helped the progress of small farmers and workers. The military Government under a moderate leader, General Policarpo Paz García, has promised that free presidential elections will be held shortly.

For Guatemala, the main problem with this ordinarily affable neighbor is that Honduras has been serving as a conduit for military supplies to leftist guerrillas in El Salvador and in Guatemala as well. Although the Honduran Government has promised to clamp down on the illegal traffic, it is not likely to be restrained effectively.

Costa Rica, which has taken a more active position on arms supplies to leftist rebels, has drawn Guatemalan resentment and antagonism. The liberal-democratic Costa Rican Government officially aided the Sandinistas in the Nicaraguan revolution by offering its territory as a staging area for across-the-border raids. Also, when civil war broke out in El Salvador, Costa Rican arms sellers began to supply the leftist guerrillas there.

The economies of all five nations of the Central American community have been seriously affected by the political upheavals that began in 1979. One institution threatened is the Central American Common Market, which was formed in 1960 to provide for free trade among the countries. Except for certain common agricultural exports like coffee, sugar, and cotton, most goods and commodities could be moved throughout the zone without customs duties or other trade barriers. Because of international tensions, bickerings, and border disputes, the Central American Common Market has suffered many disruptions in the past. But it appears to face even greater obstacles, if not dissolution, in the 1980's.

As the new decade began, Guatemala's relations with its other isthmian neighbors—Panama and Belize—were cool at best.

The Carter administration's Panama Canal treaties, relinquishing control of the canal to Panama in the year 2000, had been opposed by conservatives in the United States and by the Guatemalan Government as well. Guatemalan right-wingers fear that the way might thus be opened for Communist penetration into the region, particularly since Panama—like Costa Rica—officially supported the Sandinista revolution in Nicaragua.

Regarding Belize, Guatemala's claim to that territory remains very much alive and provides a strong nationalistic issue for Guatemala's political leaders. The population of Belize is largely black, Protestant, and English-speaking, and it includes minority groups of East Indians, Syrians, Lebanese, and Orientals. Yet despite the many racial, ethnic, religious, and linguistic differences between the two countries, Guatemala feels it must control Belize, particularly since it was granted its independence by Great Britain in 1981. Left to its own, Guatemalan officials fear that Belize might become the target of Communist infiltration.

A major influence on Central America is, of course, Mexico. There are some similarities but also many differences between Guatemala and its northern neighbor, and Guatemala cannot be viewed as a "miniature Mexico." Although Mexico itself has not achieved true democracy or an egalitarian social structure, it has —under President José López Portillo—befriended liberal and leftist governments in the region, including Sandinist Nicaragua and Castro's Cuba. As a result, there has been a growing chilliness in relations, with Guatemala viewing Mexico as both two-faced and domineering.

Contemporary Guatemala is both similar to and different from its Central American neighbors. Although it played a historic leadership role in the region, its position today is somewhat isolated. It sees itself, with pride, as the only remaining stable nation that staunchly champions the cause of anti-Communism.

Mexico's President José López Portillo at the United Nations in 1979

Yet the very rigidity of its conservatism may well prove its downfall.

Like most of its neighbors, Guatemala has a large have-not population that has been emboldened by desperate need and rising expectations to make demands for change. However, unlike the other have-nots of the isthmus, Guatemala's large Indian population has been slow to put forward its claims. Bonded to its Mayan past, unassimilated into the mainstream of the society, it too has been a conservative force.

150

Now that picture is changing. Perhaps, as Guatemalan Government officials assert, outside influences have been responsible in part. But whatever the impetus, there is a growing awareness and militancy. Indians and other small farmers claim their land rights; workers want an adequate minimum wage, decent working conditions, and a free labor movement.

Guatemalan right-wingers have found it convenient to label all those with opposing views as agitators and to denounce them as Communists, thus outlawing them and their efforts. As a result, no recognized political group has so far been able to establish a moderate, centrist program for reform.

Why is Guatemala important to the United States and how does it view that nation? The United States wants to see trade and tourism flourish between the two countries. But, above all, it is anxious to see Guatemala avoid a fierce revolutionary upheaval that might usher in a Communist regime, perhaps as extreme as that of Cuba.

During the administration of Jimmy Carter, the United States Government criticized Guatemala for its illegal arrests, political murders, and other violations of human rights. When military funding from the United States was cut off, Guatemala turned to the repressive government of Argentina and the racist government of South Africa for financial aid. President Ronald Reagan, who took office in 1981, was less critical of authoritarian right-wing governments, and Guatemala hoped that the United States would support it in its fight against the left, both at home and elsewhere in Central America. Such support, however, might well lead to stepped-up guerrilla activity that would polarize the nation, resulting in open warfare, a sharp swing to the left, and possibly the very outcome that the United States has been anxious to avoid.

Guatemala cannot offer itself as a key to stability in Central

151

America, as two of its neighbors have already entered a period of political turmoil and change. On the contrary, its own stability is in danger, and clearly it would do best not to seek help from either the conservative leaders of the United States or such prosperous but authoritarian regimes as those of Argentina and South Africa. Instead it must seek, with compassion and intelligence, to work out its own problems in order to defuse the nation's terrifying potential for civil war.

Guatemala is the most richly endowed country on the Central American isthmus. Culturally, its living past is proud and vibrant, and it merits preservation at all costs. Socially and politically, Guatemala's past has also continued to assert itself strongly. But the time has long since come for modifications, for

Indians, symbols of Guatemala's living past,
sit contemplatively on the steps of the church at Chichicastenango

real understanding of the need for social reform, and for an end to political repression and political violence.

It is to be hoped that, before it is too late, changes guaranteeing human dignity and freedoms will be made from within so that the treasure that is Guatemala can endure.

Bibliography

Benson, Elizabeth P. *The Maya World*. Rev. ed. New York: Crowell, 1977.

Colby, Benjamin N., and Berghe, Pierre L. van den. *Ixil Country: A Plural Society in Highland Guatemala*. Berkeley: University of California Press, 1969.

Dombrowski, John, and others. *Area Handbook for Guatemala*. Washington, D.C.: Government Printing Office, 1970.

Jones, Chester Lloyd. *Guatemala Past and Present*. Reissued. New York: Russell and Russell, 1966.

Kelsey, Vera, and Osborne, Lilly de Jongh. *Four Keys to Guatemala*. 2d rev. ed. New York: Funk and Wagnalls, 1978.

Rodríguez, Mario. *Central America*. Englewood Cliffs, N.J.: Prentice-Hall, Inc., 1965.

Stephens, John L. *Incidents of Travel in Central America, Chiapas, and Yucatan*. 2d ed. New Brunswick, N.J.: Rutgers University Press, 1949.

West, Robert C., and Augelli, John P. *Middle America: Its Lands and Peoples*. Englewood Cliffs, N.J.: Prentice-Hall, Inc., 1966.

Woodward, Ralph Lee, Jr. *Central America: A Nation Divided*. New York: Oxford University Press, 1976.

Index

indicates illustration

Index

*indicates illustration

ABOUT THE AUTHOR

Lila Perl was born and educated in New York City, and she holds a B.A. degree from Brooklyn College. In addition, she has taken graduate work at Teachers College, Columbia University, and at the School of Education, New York University. She is the author of a number of books for adults and for children, both fiction and nonfiction. Several of them concern life in other lands. In preparation for writing them, Miss Perl travels extensively in the country, doing firsthand research and taking many photographs. Her husband, Charles Yerkow, is also a writer, and they live in Beechhurst, New York.